THE 5TH SIMPLE STEP TO YOUR PERFECT HOME, JOB, AND LIFE

How Less Becomes More at Work

Ivan Kuznietsov

Amazon Kindle Direct Publishing

REVIEW

"This book delivers the tools and mindsets you need to rid the clutter that's piling on your desk, clogging your calendar, and infiltrating your personal networks. If you want joy in life, the place to begin is "The 5th Simple Step to Your Perfect Home, Job, and Life." —*Angela T., Lecturer*

"Ivan Kuznietsov understands something very important about life and work: many times, the key to success comes from subtracting, not adding. For anyone looking to bring more focus to their office and career, this book you've been waiting for." — *Daniel B., Ph.D*

"Sometimes, finding purpose at work isn't easy. It takes inner work. But it might feel a bit more like play thanks to the practical insights from the author of this book." —*Adam C., Barista*

* * * * *

"A guide to finding meaning at work. Full of psychological wisdom and practical tips. I like it!" —*Alex P., Project Manager*

* * * * *

"This book will help you be focused, waste less time, and lead others." —*Margaret S., Recruiter*

ABOUT THE BOOK

A certified World Class Manufacturing (WCM/Lean) Instructor shows you how to step-by-step turn your work routine into a process of calm, purpose, and inspiration.

"The 5th Simple Step to Your Perfect Home, Job, and Life" is the fifth book of the *5 Steps* series. Ivan Kuznietsov gives us a simplifying guide, which focuses on improving our work performance and the psychology of involving our colleagues in the change process. He also offers practical tips for integrating mindfulness into our working process and dealing with bosses. So the purpose of this book is not just to create a more organized working space. Instead, this book helps us to turn our job into a launching pad for a more mindful and fulfilling life. With detailed guidance, this book will help you quickly start decluttering process at your work and enjoy the unique atmosphere of mindful working.

In this book, Ivan helps you:
* Realize 4 keys point to finding
more happiness at work
* Integrate mindfulness into your workday
* Accomplish more with a 3-Item To-Do List
* Use The 10-Minute Rule
* Impress your new colleagues
* Bring peace when you deal with a difficult boss
* Find 10 simple ways to help you say "No" politely
* And much more

Are you ready to get rid of clutter, mess, and stress
at work? With the right guidance, the journey
to your perfect job is very straightforward. And
just now is the best time to take the next step.

ABOUT THE
BOOK SERIES

The 5 Steps book series is designed to inspire readers to pursue their greatest passions during the journey of simplifying work and life.

Ivan Kuznietsov, a certified World Class Manufacturing (WCM/Lean) Instructor, inspires people to make their homes, jobs and lives perfect with the simple 5 Steps simplifying method. It does not boldly require anyone to change their life overnight. Instead, it encourages each reader to discover their own journey and the far-reaching benefits of the refocused life. Moreover, Ivan Kuznietsov takes the decluttering process to a whole new level, promising that if you properly simplify and organize your home and workplace once, you'll not have to do it for a long time. As a result, the 5 Steps Method, with its straightforward step-by-step approach, leads to lasting results.

The *5 Steps* series includes the following books:
* The 1st Simple Step to Your Perfect Home: How to Methodologically Sort Through All Items, Keep Important, and Get Rid of Unnecessary
* The 2nd Simple Step to Your Perfect Home: How to Methodically Put All Necessary Items in the Optimal Places and Organize Everyday Life
* The 3rd Simple Step to Your Perfect Home: How to Mindfully Clean Your House, Digital, Mind, and Life
* The 4th Simple Step to Your Perfect Home: How to Turn Your House Cleaning Routine into a Joyful Family Tradition
* The 5th Simple Step to Your Perfect Home, Job, and Life: How Less Becomes More at Work

The beauty of the 5 Steps Method isn't in what it takes away—it's in what it gives to you. With practical suggestions to personalize your home and workplace, Ivan shows you why organizing possessions is the best way to maximize life.

CONTENTS

Tasking

Dedicated to everyone who supports and encourages me on my writing journey. Your inspiration made this book possible. May this book continue to inspire others to change for the better.

CHAPTER 1: BEFORE YOU TAKE THE FIFTH STEP

C hoosing to simplify at home can feel like a daunting task a first. But once you begin, you notice the positive effects that seem to ripple through every area of your life. The one place that can be a bit more challenging, however, is work.

We often have very different expectations and constraints in our work lives. But whether you are self-employed, working from home, or in a more structured environment, there are simple ways to make changes that can affect your satisfaction and promotion.

I held several different jobs before I decided to publish books, and much of my journey has coincided with my need for more structure and simplicity in my work life. Even before I started writing, I knew that so many of my personal habits affected my happiness at work. Eventually, I learned that writing was the best route for me for that time, but this came after a great deal of soul searching. As a result, becoming a self-publisher forced me to take a hard look at how I view work and its place in my life. And I want to share with you what I have learned.

But first, let me tell you a little about myself. My name is Ivan. I am a certified World Class Manufacturing (WCM/Lean) Instructor. And now you are reading the fifth and the final book in the *5 Steps* series.

If you started your acquaintance with the 5 Step Method with this book, then everything is going as it should. I have written books in such a way that the readers can always easily read my books in free order.

If you want to learn the 5 Steps Method from the very beginning and consistently go through all the steps together with the instructor (I'm at your service), then you will find links to my previous four books at the end of this one. (See the chapter, "Also by Ivan Kuznietsov.")

As I mentioned in the previous books, my journey begins in Ukraine. One morning when I was a kid and decluttered my room, the next thought visit me: "Maybe to stop making a mess is better than constantly declutter my room?"

Then I immediately realized something needed to change. Many of my belongings were not adding value to my life. Instead, sometimes things only distracted from it.

Soon my family and I began revision and removing our unnecessary possessions from our home. We embarked on an intentional journey to organize things in our home once and for a long time.

As a result, we discovered more free space, more time, more energy, more money, and less stress. This gave us more opportunities to pursue our greatest passions: relationships, friends, and hobbies. But I decided not to stop on it.

After graduation from the Metallurgical Academy in 2014, I got a job in the Service for Operational Improvements and Improving Efficiency of Business Processes. This was my dream job. I was in the right place at the right time. But there was still a lot of work ahead.

In 2016, after another two years of study, I received a certificate of World Class Manufacturing Instructor. Soon, together with the team, I reached the Silver Award for WCM system implementation.

Then I had an idea: "Maybe it is time to adapt all the knowledge gained at my job to everyday life?" And I decided to write about it. That's how the *5 Steps* book series was born. My goal is to teach you how to integrate best Lean practices into everyday life and work, but not the way you knew it up to this moment.

*Lean—in short, Lean methodology is a way of optimizing the resources, people, effort, and energy. It is based on two guiding tenets: continuous improvement and respect for people.

It does not require anyone to become a minimalist or something like this. We're all different, and each of us tries to make the most of this journey called life. So I encourage each reader to discover their own way and the far-reaching benefits of the Lean approach.

Now let's talk a little about the origin of the 5 Steps Method (it is also often called shortly "5S"). Initially, the 5S system was developed in Japan and was identified as the fundamental Lean method to improve manufacturing processes.

5S is a workplace organization method that includes five consecutive steps:

1. Sort.
2. Set in order.
3. Shine.
4. Standardize.

5. Sustain.

The 5S Method describes how to organize a workspace for efficiency and effectiveness by identifying and storing the items used, maintaining the equipment, and sustaining the order. The decision-making process usually comes from a dialogue about standardization, which builds understanding among people of how they should do their work for the best safety and productivity.

But 5S is more than just an element of improving businesses and everyday life. 5S is a lifestyle. So my goal is to clear the 5Steps Method of the complex terminology and make it accessible to all readers.

I repeat: 5S is a fundamental method that drives further change for the better. If you miss this step, it is very difficult to organized work and everyday life. The 5S Method will help you start taking the first right steps towards changes in your life.

This 5th book of the *5 Steps* book series will focus more on the fifth step—sustain. I will teach you how to declutter your workspace, involve your colleagues or employees in the decluttering process at work, implement a culture of simplicity in your company, treat your job with respect, and some more.

So let's take the fifth step towards your favorite job and a new life.

IVAN KUZNIETSOV

CHAPTER 2: WHY WE WORK

At its very core, your work is essential to all of us. Back in the beginning, families were responsible for accomplishing everything for their existence: build, sew, hunt, farm, cook, clean, etc. Until one day, when somebody noticed their family was better at building than farming and decided to barter with a neighboring family. "If we build an extra house that you can live in, will you grow extra food and give it to us?"

Something like that, our understanding of work was born. Both benefited from the arrangement: stronger homes were built, and better food was grown. As a result, all of society benefited. In this way, each individual was able to pursue contributions in their area of giftedness and passion.

"Hide not your talents, they for use were made." — Benjamin Franklin

But somewhere along the way, we lost our inner focus. We no longer worked to benefit others but ourselves. Our work became selfish. Work became that thing through which we make money so that we could do the other things we really wanted to do. As a result, quality work became something to avoid or shortcut if possible.

Meanwhile, we still need our talents and abilities. We still need to work hard and do it well. Our quality work contributes to the good of society and moves us forward. Society desperately needs our contribution. It makes us better as people and enriches our lives.

So, please don't view your work as something only to be endured or avoided. Instead, just rethink your work. Regain focus and motivation to use your passions and abilities to contribute well to a society in need of them.

Develop your talents. Study your craft. Utilize your strengths. And encourage others. Seek honest compensation, not riches. Work hard and enjoy it. And at the end of this day, we will all be better because of it.

CHAPTER 3: DO WORK YOU LOVE

C onfucius, an ancient Chinese philosopher, is credited with saying:

> *"Choose a job you love, and you will never have to work a day in your life."*

Whether you are 18, 29, or 70, you are making choices now that will chart the course for the rest of your life. And those who choose to embrace the idea of decluttering life open up the rest of his or her life to endless possibilities—including picking a passion as a career.

Somebody who decides to mindfully live with less clutter has less need to hold a certain level of income. As a result, they can choose whatever career path they most wish. Moreover, their decision does not have to be dictated by income level only.

While there is nothing wrong with earning money, when your salary package can be removed from the career-choice equation, you are free to choose your career based on other factors—such as "something I really want to do." So declutter your life—choose work you love.

CHAPTER 4: WHY IT'S IMPORTANT TO WORK WITH MEANING

Some people choose simple life as a means to escape work. While you understand the appeal, you are not one of them.

As for me, I enjoy hard work. I find happiness, joy, and meaning in it. And I believe, without a doubt in my mind: Those who feel the most fulfilled at the end of their lives are those who have chosen to work hard during it.

Now, just to be clear, I am not advocating to be very busy just to be very busy. I am just advocating for the importance of doing your work (whether paid or unpaid) in a focused and deliberate way, putting your whole self into it. Doing the best you can, to accomplish the most you can, with the life you've got.

But if one has chosen simplicity as a lifestyle, where do we find the motivation to learn how to work hard? After all, if we are content to own less, what is the point of hard work and striving for success?

If the goal of our work isn't to earn more and more money so we can buy bigger and bigger houses and fancier and more expensive cars, then what's the point? If we've chosen to measure life's success in more meaningful terms than material possessions, why would we choose to work hard?

There are, actually, countless reasons. But, consider these seven, just to get started:

1. Work forces personal development.

Work, by its very nature, presents us with challenges and growth opportunities. It requires us to improve, develop and become better versions of ourselves. And the more we grow, the better at work we get.

2. Work is fulfilling, in and of itself.

In my opinion, there are few joys in life more satisfying than laying down in the evening with tired legs after a productive day. To know I gave my energy to something meaningful is a fantastic feeling and fulfilling in itself.

3. Work hard at work to get benefits in life.

We learn important life lessons when we give ourselves over to hard work: determination, attentiveness, responsibility, problem-solving, and self-motivation all come to mind. These lessons, in turn, serve us in other areas like health, relationships, hobbies, etc.

4. Work hard to make the most of your hours.

Each new day brings with it an important choice: either we fill it with our best, or we allow it to slip away. There is no other option, and the hours are going to pass anyway. So choosing to work hard makes the most of them. But please note: I am not discounting the importance of rest or balance. Instead, I advise you to find your own balance of rest.

5. Our work brings benefits to society.

Our work contributes to the good of our society. It can serve others, it enriches peoples' lives, and it moves everyone forward. Whether we are bagging groceries, analyzing stocks, delivering mail, or managing other workers, we can view our work as an act of love to the people we serve.

6. Working hard keeps our lives occupied with important matters.

Living an unoccupied life is a recipe for stress. Instead, choosing to fill our time and energy with things that bring value to others helps keep us from selfish and foolish decisions with idle time.

7. Hard work is an example to our kids.

When we strive to do our best work each day—our kids take notice. And among the greatest character traits, all people hope to pass on to children the importance of working hard on things that matter.

There is value in hard work, and the 5 Steps Method does not remove its inherent value. On the contrary, in my opinion, it brings its inherent value in sharper focus.

Before ending this chapter, allow me to briefly speak to those of you disengaged at work—those who no longer find any joy in their specific role and want nothing more than to escape it.

I understand that not every job is enjoyable, and feeling motivated to work hard comes easier to someone who looks forward to punching in the clock each morning or evening. However, sometimes, we are required to do work we do not enjoy. If that's you, please remember, your unenjoyment of work does not diminish the inherent value in it.

If you are working a job you hate to provide for your family—you are doing a noble thing. And working hard at it, in the place you are now, is your most important step out of it.

CHAPTER 5: OUR LOVE AND HATE RELATIONSHIP WITH WORK

The statistics concerning work in America tell an enlightening story. On the one hand, people hate work. On the other hand, people can't seem to get enough of it.

For the most part, Americans are dissatisfied with their jobs:

* 70% of employed Americans are disengaged from their work.

* 18% of workers are actively disengaged—meaning they aren't just unhappy; they are busy acting out their unhappiness.

* 74% of employed workers would consider a new job opportunity if one was presented.

* Americans count down the years to retirement at age 65, and CNN defines early retirement as the ultimate "American Dream."

So, Americans are not happy with their work and do not enjoy it. But they refuse to slow down and take any break from it:

* Compared with other industrialized nations, U.S. workers rank 1st in hours worked (1,800 hours annually).

* The typical American middle-income family works an average of 11 more hours a week in 2006 than it did in 1979.

* 53% of adults check work messages at least once a day over the weekend.

* Some Americans struggle to find even one day of rest each week.

* Americans leave a half billion vacation days unused each year.

These statistics paint an interesting picture of love and hate relationship with work worldwide: People don't like their jobs but refuse to spend less time at them. So why is this the case?

Most likely, there are a number of reasons. Sometimes, our legitimate financial needs require us to work hard for long hours. Sometimes, our jobs require us to be on-call and available at any moment. Other times, our employers simply do not provide us the right type of flexibility.

But I think there is something deeper. After all, all of this is happening in many productive and wealthy nations. So why then, given our vast supply of nowadays opportunities, do we work such long hours in jobs we hate?

If we could discover the deeper reason for this discontent, we could find relief in both areas: both a greater appreciation for our job and more space for rest. But the real reason we have such a love and hate relationship with work in our society is that our motivation for it is unconscious. We do our work for the wrong reward.

Typically, we do our jobs simply for the purpose of earning a paycheck at the end of the day/week/month. Work is that thing we do through which we make money so we can do all the other things we really want to do in our lives.

But money as a means to fulfillment and happiness will always fall short. It will never fully satisfy the longings of our hearts. In their own right, power, reputation, and fame never satisfy either.

When money is the main reward, we can never earn enough. So we are always left desiring just a little bit more.

This is a real problem with our modern understanding of work. If we are only doing it for the sake of the paycheck, it will never be enough. In that case, we will always be left searching for more —putting in just a few more hours, heading back to the office on another Saturday morning, and skipping another day of vacation.

Do we work because we love our jobs and find real fulfillment in them? Not always. We do it because we believe the paycheck makes it all worthwhile (or at least, a little bit bigger paycheck will make it all worthwhile). But, as statistics show, it never does.

We were designed to work for something greater than money, possessions, and property. Instead, view work as a contribution to others—this is a great reward. Our work can contribute to the good of society. In that case, it moves us forward. It makes us better as employees and humans. It enriches our hearts and lives.

Whether we are delivering mail, bagging groceries, sweeping streets, or managing others—we can view our hard work as an act of love to the people we serve. And when we change our motivation, we discover work is not something to be avoided. It is meaningful.

So please don't view your work as something to be endured or avoided. Also, don't view it merely as a means to a paycheck. Change your focus today and develop a deeper appreciation for the contribution you are making (or find a job that will). This will al-ways result in a new love relationship with work.

CHAPTER 6: IMPORTANT THINGS TO CONSIDER IF YOU HATE YOUR JOB

I know one man who is really unhappy with his job. It's not that he is having a bad week or a hard day. Instead, it's been months of dissatisfaction, feeling unfulfilled, and wanting something more.

With his daily commute, office hours, and the work that lingers after work, he spends at least 11 hours a day devoted to his job. And that doesn't count all of the time and energy he spends thinking about how much he hates his job. He agonizes over the fact that he is doing something that makes him miserable and something he doesn't care about.

He is compromising his dreams, happiness, and relationships for a paycheck. He is overwhelmed and stuck in fear, resistance, and uncertainty. This is a true-life story, and if you aren't in this situation, it might sound dramatic, but it's real. Unfortunately, it's also real for so many people, and it was my reality too.

My friend is stuck, and I thought the advice I shared with him might be helpful if you hate your job too. So there are 7 important things to consider if you hate your job:

1. You are not what you do.

If you measure your worth by what you earn, how you contribute financially, or what your title is, you may lack clarity on what you really have to offer. You are worth so much more than what you do or what you earn just because of who you really are. Your value as being a person is not tied to your job.

2. When you understand yourself first, you can better serve everyone around you.

Maybe you tell yourself that you are staying at your job to support your family. But aside from dollars in the bank, are you really supporting your family? How are you taking care of your body, heart, and mind so that you can offer your best self to support the people you love? Remember: Your work style and lifestyle are deeply connected. So they can support each other, or they don't.

3. Interests trump skills.

Just because you are good at what you do doesn't mean you are supposed to be doing it all the time. But when you become mindfully interested in something, you can learn how to do it well. And over time, these skills only improve.

4. When your desire for peace, love, and happiness becomes greater than your fear of uncertainty, you'll quit.

Hating your work isn't enough. You need to love something more than you hate your work. Instead of waiting for the enough is enough, stomp your feet and scream "I quit" moment, look for a quiet awareness of what matters most in your life. Realize the temporary nature of things and believe that everything that is done is for the best.

5. Your next job might not be your dream job.

If you want to quit your job until your dream job comes along, consider that there might be something in between. When you are overwhelmed and feel stuck, it can be challenging to know what you want to do next. Now all of your energy is spent on survival mode, so a stop over between the job you hate and the job you'll love can be a beautiful respite. So if you want to take things to the next level, keep in mind that the next level doesn't always match your dreams.

6. Until you have clarity, ask for help.

Find people that will support you as you go through this process. Not co-workers who hate their job too, but someone who can see the bigger picture. Read literature about successful people and get inspired by their examples. After all, every person in his life experienced something similar. You are not alone.

7. Be yourself and believe in the best.

If you do not deceive yourself, then you do not have to deceive others. Be honest with yourself. Trust your intuition. Work on yourself, and then the opportunities will meet you. Remember this.

I sincerely hope that these tips will help you find your hidden resources and make the right decision. You just need to do a little work on yourself first.

CHAPTER 7: SOMETIMES YOU DON'T REALLY HAVE TO QUIT YOUR JOB

You don't have to quit your job to live a free life. If you read blogs about mindful living, you might notice that it seems like everyone quits their job, travels the world, writes a book, and lives the life of their dreams.

But living your life on purpose does not require you to quit your job, have a blog, travel the world, or even practice yoga (however, a mindful life looks different for each of us).

"Make your life about creating the good instead of escaping the bad."

Even if your job isn't your dream, it might be the way you provide health insurance for your family, pay off debt and save for vacations. But can you still start working towards your dream and make a slow, deliberate change to recreate your life? Without a doubt, yes! Does that mean you have to quit your job and declare your freedom to be a success? Absolutely not!

If you like your job but are feeling stressed, try the next things:

* Declutter and organize your desk/workspace.

* Commit to a lunch hour

* Leave your workspace for a short walk

* Take a day off

* Exercise

* Try new master-class or learn a new skill

* Volunteer

Celebrate with people that did quit their day jobs, but don't be discouraged from living more mindfully if you work for someone else. If you don't like your job, start planning right now. What would it take to find another good job or to work for your-self? It might take months or more to be in a posi-tion to make that kind of change, so why not start your search and make your plan today.

If you plan a new career, do the following:

* Be consistent and organized

* Pay off your debt

* Determine how much money you really need to fund your mindful life

* Start an emergency fund

* Take classes or educate yourself if you are con-sidering a new field

* Hang out with other people doing what you want to do

* Be patient but act quickly if necessary

Only you know what's best for you and your fam-ily. And you know that what's best can change over time. What is best for you today may be different in the next month. What is best for you might not be best for anyone else.

By paying off your debt, reducing your expenses, and craving less instead of more, you can start to make choices based on something other than the almighty dollar. And the mindful your life be-comes, the easier it will be to define the next step.

IVAN KUZNIETSOV

CHAPTER 8:
KEYS POINT TO
FINDING MORE
HAPPINESS
AT WORK

In our world today, we are overwhelmed with promises to quit our responsibilities and jobs and chase our wishes and dreams. We are told that we deserve to be happy and that it will eventually happen if we buy enough things. We are told to work for the weekend and plan our next vacation. But why can't we be happy with the life we have today, right now?

We live in a world that prizes leisure over labor and longs for a "four-hour workweek." Sadly, like many things in our world, this promise is an illusion. The truth is you don't have to hate or leave your job. Instead, work can become a source of fulfillment for you if you choose to see it the right way.

As I spoke with people who had found their callings, I learned several lessons. Here are four of them:

1. Realize your whole life is a form of work.

Whether or not you have a day job, you go to work every single day. You clean up the house or watch the kids. You mow the lawn or go shopping. Whether you are retired or just beginning your career, you are working every day, whether it's at an office or at home.

So we all have important work to do—and that work is our life. Our work is not just one great thing we did. It is more like a body of work that you are constantly contributing to every single day.

In that respect, we all get to decide what kind of work we do and how much we enjoy it. But, of course, there are some things that are within our control, like our current circumstances. So your job is to learn to let go of what you can't control and embrace what you can.

2. The choice is always yours.

One important lesson about being happier with

your work (and life) is learning to make trade-offs. It's the dream of many people to want more of everything: more time, more money, more stuff. But you can't have all three of those all at once and every time.

So decide what's most important to you at this moment. Realize that you can do almost anything you want in life but not everything. And if you're not doing what you want, you can quit. But that choice will have consequences. You can also stay where you are, and there is a cost to that as well. Just realize that the choice is always yours.

However, there is something beautiful about not getting everything you thought you wanted. Sometimes constraints create contentment. Because in those constraints, you realize what's really matters.

3. The point is not what you do but how you do it.

Hating your job won't make you any happier. We don't have to hate our work even if that work isn't ideally suited to us. Everyone I met who found their calling in life ended up doing something that challenged and surprised them. This means that connecting to your inner purpose is more about perspective than circumstance.

During World War II, Austrian psychiatrist Viktor Frankl discovered an essential lesson about human happiness:

*"When we are no longer able to change a situation,
we are challenged to change ourselves."*

Frankl learned this lesson from living for years in a Nazi concentration camp. Everything was taken from him: his family, his work, and his well-being. And yet, he realized there was one freedom he could never lose: his.

So, if you choose to change your perspective, how things look will begin to change too. And you don't need to win the lottery to find contentment. In fact, sometimes, the very things we think will liberate us will actually only further prison us.

The easiest way to do the work you love is to start loving how you do. This is a choice we all have. So let's stop making work the enemy.

4. Do better work, and the result will become more enjoyable.

The best way to enjoy your work is to become better at it. So it should be no surprise that we find greater fulfillment in activities that we are skilled at doing. But how much this is true is startling!

In the Stanford Center on Longevity, psychologists study what makes people live longer and happier lives. And what they found was that people who continue to learn enjoy their work more and actually live longer.

Education, according to this study, is the single most significant predictor of lifespan. So you want to live longer? Be happier at work? Start to learn a new skill or get better at the one you have. And why not start with the place where you probably already spend eight hours a day, five days a week?

Once we reach a basic level of proficiency, work that was once tedious may now be enjoyable. In addition, mastering any skill makes the activity intrinsically more motivating. So if you are struggling to want to go to work in the first place, just try doing better work.

Once you understand these four truths, your attitude towards work will change. And after your attitude to work changes, so will the results.

CHAPTER 9: A 7-STEP PATH TO ENJOYING YOUR WORK

P eople spend a significant amount of their life working. So it is vital to think thoughtfully and intentionally about it:

* The average person will spend 20% of their life at work.

* This statistic factors in 21 years of preparing for work and 13 years afterward (retirement).

* During our actual years of working (ages 21-67), this percentage goes up to 25-30% based on a typical 40-45 hour/week.

* Subtracting sleep, on average, we spend 33% of our waking hours working.

I know countless people who are happy with their work. They all find meaning, significance, and joy in it. Additionally, I have met many people who are unhappy with their job and choose to spend an additional percentage of their life complaining about it.

Interestingly enough, these differences in attitudes have little to do with the actual work being done. In fact, two people in the same field can have completely different responses to the same work.

"We often miss opportunity because it's dressed in overalls and looks like work."—Thomas A. Edison

This idea is very helpful because it means enjoying work has less to do with your actual job and more to do with your attitude towards it. Changing our attitude towards work is often far more straightforward than changing jobs. It also means that you can be happy with your work today. You can find joy and fulfillment in what you do. And often, this can come with a simple change in thinking.

A 7-Step Path to Enjoying Your Work:

1. Realize you were born to contribute to this world.

Whether by creation or evolution, humans are born

to work. This is an essential part of our nature. It explains our endless drive to grow as individuals and as a society. It explains the deep internal satisfaction we experience when completing a task. It also makes sense of the positive emotions we experience when resting after a productive day of work. And it also may help us understand why some studies indicate early retirement has an adverse impact on physical and mental health.

The realization that we were born to contribute to this world is an important first step in finding fulfillment in our work—even though "work" looks different for each of us. If we are designed to accomplish our work, it is not something to be avoided. Instead, it is something to be sought and enjoyed.

2. Understand that work takes place in an imperfect world.

Our world is imperfect because we exist in reality, full of people who often fall short. Though we each have an ingrained desire to accomplish good for the sake of others, in fact, we usually function with selfish desires and intentions. So these imperfections always lead to less-than-ideal working conditions. As a result, work includes overbearing bosses, under-resourced projects, deadlines, tasks we do not enjoy, stress, and very often, anxiety.

The realization that these imperfections will always be present in our workplace allows us to accept them and move forward. Now just to be clear, this current reality does not mean we don't fight for equality and justice when appropriate. But it does mean we can stop looking for joy in the perfect work environment because it doesn't exist in the outside world. Instead, we have to open our minds to finding joy in our inner world in order to share it through our work.

3. Use work to supply provisions for yourself and your family.

In its simplest definition, work is an ancient bartering tool. We work our jobs in exchange for money (sometimes goods). This money is then given to other people in exchange for building shelter, producing clothing, growing food, or discovering new medicine to keep us healthy. This is the law of life in society. Because of work, we are freed to spend our hours doing what we love and are good at. In exchange, we receive money (goods) to trade with someone else who used their giftedness to create something we need.

But looking for shortcuts (dishonest gain or unnecessary dependence on others) to supply provisions is often a foolish direction for life. An honest relationship is the natural goal of work. And this is the prescribed means of providing for those who are dependent upon us.

4. Notice how your work contributes to the common good.

If the goal of our work is to contribute well to society in exchange for provision, then our work ought to benefit society as much as possible. We should spend our time producing a benefit for others. We should grow healthy food, produce quality clothing, build strong shelter, create beautiful art, develop new life-enhancing technology, research medicine to prolong life, educate others, intentionally parent children, govern society honestly, or any other countless opportunities to contribute to the common good of our neighbor and our community.

This idea results in 2 possible outcomes:

First, it forces us to view work differently. It allows us to wake up every morning with a positive attitude and opens up the door to finding new joy in our role.

And second, this truth forces us to find new work. If for whatever reason, we do not believe our job is contributing good to society, we must find a new one. No dollar amount can ever equal the satisfaction and joy experienced in contributing good to the world around us because this is the purpose of life.

5. Work ethically.

Work done ethically and honestly with proper balance will always result in more enjoyment. The same principle holds true to every aspect of life.

6. Let go of the pursuit of riches.

While fair compensation should always be sought with both humility and pride, the pursuit of riches and wealth as an end goal is always a losing battle. Prosperity will never fully satisfy, and we will always be left searching for more. People who view their work as only a means to get rich very often fall into temptation, harmful behavior, and foolish desires. But when we replace the desire to get rich with a more life-fulfilling desire to receive fair compensation, we open our hearts to find peace in our paychecks and greater value in our work.

7. Humbly accept fair compensation.

We each have the skills and talents this world needs. Other people are willing to compensate us in exchange for them. Therefore, we ought to work hard at proudly developing our craft and humbly learning as much as we can from other people. It is also wise to discipline ourselves around the improvement of our skills and talents. The greater we develop our skills, the greater we are worth to others. And the greater we are worth to others, the more honest compensation we should receive for providing them.

The intentional understanding of the ideas above provides great freedom for us to enjoy work on a whole new level. Indeed, may each of us find greater value and fulfillment in our work and job. And in so doing, may we increase joy in this essential aspect of our lives.

CHAPTER 10: WHEN LESS BECOMES MORE AT WORK

Any work environment is comparable to a battlefield when it comes to accomplishing duties. Too much work to handle, and you'll feel like a lone soldier battling against hundreds of opponents. So you have to choose your battles, or you risk a high probability of defeat.

Listed below are a few simple tips that can help you become more productive by doing less:

1. Work smarter, not work harder.

While hardworking lends a positive tone to one's character, being always busy does not necessarily translate to productivity. And while one may exert much effort on a task, the work done may not be too efficient to arrive at the desired results.

The best tip for maximizing productivity is to optimize your energy. Save most of your inner energy on the more important things to do, and stop wasting it on dilly-dally. Not only will you save yourself from mental and physical fatigue, but you will also find yourself with some extra time to spare for relaxation at the end of your workday.

2. Stop multi-tasking.

While some of us wish to have superpowers, let's admit we're all humans. No one can handle 10 tasks at a time. So better drop most of them, and do things one at a time. Focusing on a single task at hand allows you more mental energy to accomplish important tasks in time.

3. Step by step.

You have your eyes on the desired prize. And you know exactly what to do to achieve that. But step back for a moment to reflect on how you are going to reach your goal.

Do you race ahead to the finish like the hare? Or do you go slow like the tortoise? It is best to find your inner balance to ensure that you are right on track towards accomplishment. Small, steady steps to your big goal sound better than huge, rushed ones.

Setting small goals that are a part of your larger habit goal is just an excellent way to break down a more complicated process into attainable benchmarks.

4. Set aside time to list your tasks.

The best way of breaking down your goal into smaller tasks is by identifying the immediate concerns that need to be addressed. Then, segment your workload by writing down all that needs to be done and choosing the top three tasks that you need to accomplish at the end of the day.

I have a habit of investing 10 minutes every morning to identify my top three non-negotiable activities for completion today. And I do it every day.

5. Ask for help.

When responsibilities on your table become too overwhelming for you, do not attempt to do them all by yourself and risk missing the deadline. Not ashamed to ask for help. Each of us needs some kind of help at some point in our lives. Not only will this ease your workload, but it also gives you the chance to nurture relationships with your coworkers.

6. Don't be afraid to say "no."

Do you know about the 80/20 rule? The Pareto principle states that most of the time, 80 percent of results come from 20 percent of the causes. It means 80 percent of your output is produced by only 20 percent of your efforts concerning work. Often it's okay to say "yes" to a colleague's request and accept other responsibilities. Still, too many "yes" will burden your own workload. So filter the additional commitments, and decline the less important ones.

7. Take short breaks.

Take a quick break in between tackling your to-do list to recharge your mind. I find that following the 55/5 rule makes my work more manageable, and it is the simplest and most effective productivity tool for me. It requires me to do uninterrupted work for 55 minutes, and then I spend the next 5 minutes for mental rest. Also, breaking down my work schedule in hours gives me a clearer picture of how I should go about my work.

8. Celebrate even small accomplishments.

Do you get one challenging task done in 60 minutes without checking social media? Or maybe accomplished major tasks before lunchtime? Laud yourself for each small accomplishment and get some positive reinforcement from yourself by acknowledging your small victories. There's no better motivation than knowing you are ticking off tasks on your list and progressing towards your goal.

You lessen the stress and anxiety over missed deadlines when you focus and work consistently. So reducing the energy spent on minor side activities gives you more to handle the major important ones and eventually maximize your day for productivity.

CHAPTER 11: SIMPLIFYING YOUR WORK

Here are the best ways to simplify your work —no matter where you find yourself at the moment. They have helped me, and I hope they will help you:

1. Declutter and add beauty to your workspace.

A wise person once said:

> *"A cluttered desk is a cluttered mind."*

And I must say that I agree with this point. It's impossible to think clearly about the next important task in your workday if your physical space is burdened with sticky notes, piles of paper, and yesterday's coffee mug.

There are many ways to begin implementing better systems to organize your physical workspace. I recommend you use the 5 Steps Method. Start from the very first step:

The 1st Simple Step to Your Perfect Home: How to Methodologically Sort Through All Items, Keep Important, and Get Rid of Unnecessary

From this book, you'll learn how to get started sorting things anywhere. With the 5 Steps method, you can quickly get rid of unnecessary junk and begin to appreciate what you already have.

Also, be sure to add some items to your workspace that add beauty and joy—pictures of loved ones, a plant, or awards for your achievements are all good ways to bring some peace and inspiration to a place away from home.

2. Ask yourself, "What do I really want?"

This may seem somewhat esoteric, but when it comes down to it, we only have this moment to live. Also, we will spend the majority of our lives working, so this question matters. If you find yourself in a job that you hate, it's essential to ask yourself why. Sometimes doing what we love and earning a living simply cannot coalesce into the same vocation, but not as often as we think.

What do you value the most in your life?

What work or hobby sparks joy makes the time fly by without you even noticing?

What would you do today no matter what, even if you didn't earn a dime?

These questions can help you clarify the "why" behind your work and help you see how your work can better align with who you are.

3. Find your inner strengths.

I have a rule in my life—if it's not something I'm really good at, I don't do it. Instead, I allow someone else to work according to their strengths while I am focusing on my own. This helps me execute at a much higher level than if I tried to do everything myself (believe me, I've tried).

Self-knowledge is something that can be applied in any job or position. It can give you a much deeper knowledge of "you" so that you can be sure you are doing your very best and most fulfilling work.

4. Set clear boundaries.

Boundaries often can get a bad rap because they sound so, well, unfriendly. But they are essential for creating joy and satisfaction in our work and personal life. In my case of writing, I have found that if I do not set very clear boundaries at the beginning of the day, things typically do not go well.

Statements like "I am unavailable to text after 5 pm" or "I don't typically check email on weekends" are helpful. I used to work without borders. But then I realized that if the work/life balance shifted towards work, I resent myself. But how did I know where the line was if I never realized it? So now I make sure that I realize all boundaries and expectations at the beginning of every workday.

5. Keep track of your time.

As you move throughout your workday, have you ever wondered how much time it actually took you to complete a project? Understanding where you are spending your time can be a major eye-opener.

Currently, online time trackers are a great help (and many are available for free). I find that in my work, I often put off certain projects because of overwhelming. But when I track how long they took, it was actually much less time than I expected initially. This is because we often spend more time worrying about our tasks than actually executing them. But tracking my time helps me overcome this feeling and work on the most critical items first.

No matter whether you are in a high-powered position that demands a great deal of your time or are working a few hours per week—it is vital that you make certain parts of your day off-limits. Once you decide what those boundaries are, make people known. But if you don't, no one else will.

Now I know for sure:

"There is nothing more complicated than simplifying."

Think about the meaning of this statement. But don't be afraid of this idea. Making things simpler isn't that complicated. It's harder to simplify your attitude to work. But once you are on the path of simplification, you will no longer want to leave it.

CHAPTER 12: CHOOSING BETTER WORK OVER MORE TOOLS

How much of your creativity is in your hands versus in your tools? This question comes up for me more and more often as my arsenal of work tools gets intentionally downsized. Tools are very important. Sometimes they are a means of getting the job done. And indeed, some jobs require more tools for specialized functions.

But people can become overly reliant on their tools. Photographers often believe the next lens will magically improve their photographs. Professional tennis players and golfers fidget with different rackets or clubs. And some musicians are famous for masking insufficient talent beneath a mountain of gear.

But the best musicians I've ever met can sound like themselves on any instrument. Their tone shines through from their soul because they have honed their craft and skills. It's at the heart of what I feel so many creative people miss.

So how do we know when tools are improving our work or when they are making us more inefficient instead? As people, we need to keep the quality of our work at the core of what we offer and not the tools we use to get the job done.

Sometimes projects make us think we need more tools, we start mindlessly scrolling through websites for deals. But we can regain our focus by asking ourselves a good question:

"Am I shopping for more tools or a better work?"

Marketers love to hammer our pain points, then politely offer to hold our wallets while we writhe in our inadequacy. But it is not a marketer's job to care about the quality of our work. They just want to sell us more tools (at the highest price).

It's our job to care about our work, our performance, our art, or our game. Do you want to become great and develop a signature style? First, find a few tools that are ergonomically correct, then start pursuing mastery—not in the pursuit of more tools, but in the honing of your craft. Life and work rarely benefit from layering on more complexity.

I can see now how trimming back the distractions and focusing on my craft has led to creating the product I always dreamed of. No new piece of tool or collection of fancy pens was going to improve my work. That was my responsibility and job.

So to focus on choosing better work over more tools, I have begun to embrace the following principles when it comes to my job:

1. Pare down tools to the essentials. There are some phenomenal photographers and cinematographers out there using only smartphones. Which of your primary tools create your most high-leverage output?

2. Instead of choosing more tools, choose skills. You already have everything you need for an excellent job.

3. Instead of investing money in the promise of better output, invest time, focus, and energy in creating your best impact.

4. Ask yourself the right questions. Whenever you find yourself needing an upgrade, ask: Do I really need more tools, or do I need more patient to hone my craft? It's important to address the root cause instead of adding more complexity that will only delay the impact you're trying to achieve.

5. Find motivation. Don't bail on a tool at first sight of frustration. Push through it. You may need a new tool, but maybe you just need to walk through the valley before reaching the top of the mountain.

The artist in each of us may be desperately calling out for more space, not more tools. So instead of choosing more tools, free up space for creativity at your job.

CHAPTER 13: PROVEN WAYS TO BREAK YOUR CELL DEVICE ADDICTION

These addiction statistics are quite over-whelming:

* Half of all phone pickups happen within 3 minutes of a previous one.

* The typical cell phone user touches his or her phone 2,617 times every day.

* Most people, on average, spend 3 hours and 15 minutes on their phones each day.

Most important, the impact of this usage is stag-

gering:

* The positive correlation between smartphone addiction and depression is alarming.

* Adversely impacting short-term memory and problem-solving.

* Reducing the quality of conversations.

* Resulting in more negativity, distress, and less emotional recovery in young children.

* Negatively affecting our sleep patterns.

Given the statistics and what we know to be true about cell phone usage, you may think it would be easy to put it down and walk away. But the technology addiction struggle is real. The addictive nature of mobile devices and the great internal battle is to harness the benefits of our smartphones without falling prey to their intentionally addictive power.

Nor do I miss the ironic fact that many of you are reading this very article on your phone or tablet. Phones are good and helpful. You are able to read this article right now because of it. But we know all too well they also have the potential power to become a negative presence in our life if we allow them.

So how do we keep cell phone usage in proper alignment with our work and everyday lives? What are some best tools or ideas to help us cut down on our cell phone usage?

Here is a list of seven proven ways to break cell phone addiction I have used myself:

1. Set aside one day (or week if you are on vacation).

This is the very first step and the most common approach I see among people who have taken intentional steps to curb their cell phone habit nowadays. I heard talk about it almost ten years ago. So choose one day each week (usually a Saturday and Sunday) or all week or so if you are on vacation and set your phone aside. And make a habit of it.

2. Use a 21-Day Experiment to reset your usage.

This has been the most helpful way to break my cell phone habit. When not intentionally limited, my cell phone use tends to take over more and more of my free time every day. It happens unintentionally and quietly—I don't even seem to notice how it happens.

Nine years ago, I bought a very basic mobile phone (although I already had a fancy smartphone, which I put back in the box) and used it only for calling and texting. It was a 21-day period of reset that helped me align my usage with more important pursuits in life. (According to scientists, it takes at least 21 days to get rid of old habits and develop new ones.) Since that first experiment, I have used the 21-day reset five additional times—each with great success and pleasure.

3. Change your phone settings.

Among the most often suggested ideas for reducing cell phone usage, I advise you tips and tricks by simply changing the settings on your phone. There are the most common suggested ideas:

* Delete all unused apps

* Remove distraction-based apps from your home screen

* Turn off notifications

* Set a longer passcode

In my opinion, these suggestions are something everyone should do regardless of how habitual their cell phone use is. Just because someone in the world wants to text you, email you, or tag you in a post doesn't mean they deserve your attention.

4. Use apps to bolster self-control.

There are apps for almost every issue in life. There are even some wonderful apps built to help us limit our time on our devices. And most importantly, most of these apps are free. Here are some opportunities that apps provide for a more attentive attitude to your devices:

* Set goals and track your daily progress to manage your habits.

* Lock away distracting apps for complete focus.

* Set daily usage limits on your phone or specific apps.

* Brings gamification to productivity.

5. Carry your phone in a zippered case.

In one of the most thoughtful personal stories on how to overcome cell phone addiction, it is recommended to carry a cell phone in a zippered case. Every time you want to use your phone, this brings about a mindfulness exercise and makes you ask, "what is my intention?" Then, if you really want to use the phone, set your intention for why, and remove it from the zippered case.

Zippered case is not about making your phone impossible to use. The practice is about bringing greater mindfulness to each specific use of it as opposed to mindlessly unlocking your phone every 5 minutes.

6. Put your phone away when you walk into the office (and at home too).

The simple and proven way to keep life in a healthy balance with a cell phone is to put it on the desk at the beginning of the workday. The more you physically remove the phone, the more you can build a habit of having some ability to let it go when it's possible.

Also, when you finish your day of work, put your phone in a drawer or cabinet. This is a helpful practice for all people. But I think it is especially important if you have kids or a spouse at home in need of our undivided attention.

7. Don't charge your phone near your bed.

Do you want to know the best way to keep your kids off their devices too much? Don't allow them to charge their devices in their bedroom. The same goes for you! Want to know a great way to keep yourself off your devices? Don't charge it in your bedroom.

Many of the negative effects of device overuse (poor sleep and hindered communication) can be eliminated by keeping your cell phone or other devices out of your bedroom. As with all of the items on this list, this is a step I've found personally helpful.

When used as tools to improve work, health, and life—cell phones, tablets, and other devices bring countless benefits. But when used mindlessly and unintentionally, they become a distraction from the things in work and life that matter most (in addition to the negative effects listed above). So learning how to use our devices effectively may be one of the most important life skills any of us can learn.

CHAPTER 14:
THE WEIGHT OF
DIGITAL CLUTTER

While our outer world may accurately reflect our "less is more" lifestyle, our online life paints a somewhat more cluttered picture. Anyone who has ever spent time decluttering at work will attest to the light feeling that arrives almost immediately after cleaning out the workplace. There's a sense of freedom that comes from getting rid of the clutter and tidying up. This is the feeling like you can breathe again.

But what a lot of people don't realize is that all clutter weighs on you—even if it's not taking up physical space. For example, if your email inbox is a mess, it's going to take up residence in the back of your mind until you do something about it.

There are many forms of digital clutter. At least with physical stuff, you have tangible reference points. For example, you can no longer park your car in the garage because of an overabundance of trash in it. Digital clutter, however, is both sneaky and insidious. The evidence is hidden on your office laptop and various other devices, so nobody but you is privy to the mess.

In my first-ever office job, we used USB drives to store our work. Each USB drive had a sum total of 8 gigabytes of space available. Unfortunately, our hard drives were also pathetically small, so we had no choice but to be mindful of what we saved. (The advent of the Cloud means storage space is now infinite.)

From our email inboxes and photos to bookmarked websites, eBooks, and newsletters, the extent to which we are able to hoard in virtual space is scary. Right, now let's look at the different kinds of online clutter and what we can do to lighten the virtual load.

Downloadables (eBooks, PDFS, photos, etc.)

I haven't looked at the gazillion digital photographs I have stored on my HDD. A lot of people would argue that photos are important (a link to the past, if you will). However, if you're someone who actually looks at the photos you've taken, then it makes sense to keep them organized. I paid a lot of attention to this topic in my book:

The 3rd Simple Step to Your Perfect Home: How to Mindfully Clean Your House, Digital, Mind, and Life

I love reading! I still buy paper books, but the majority of my reading happens online. There's a little problem with having instant access to millions of books—we grab whatever we come across. As for me, right now, I have 133 books on my reading device, but I've read only 69 of them.

I also have a bunch of working-related Word docs as well as PDFs (again, just in case).

Action: Sort all photos. Read all unread books on your reading device before you buy more. Check all working PDFs, Word docs, etc., by the end of the month and then delete unnecessary. Sort working documents into a system that makes sense for you.

Browser Bookmarking.

I used to bookmark the old school way. I'm used to saving websites or articles that may still be useful to me. But often, there were too many of them, which made it difficult to find really useful bookmarks.

Action: Commit yourself to check (and read if interesting) any new articles saved within a month. Do a bookmarking clean-out once a month so you can begin the new month with a clean browser.

Emails.

Emails are the new paper trail. They're the evidence we need to prove we contacted that client, placed orders, and created accounts. But somehow, we've lost the ability to discern what's really important and what's not. So it's almost easier to just keep everything (you know, just in case).

One day, I received a letter from a former colleague I haven't seen in a long time.

Subject: Cleaning up the inbox.

Message: "I am doing an inbox clean-up and wanted to check if this was still your address?"

I thought, how clever to do that every year. And, as for me, I still have emails from former colleagues I haven't worked with in more than four years. They're all neatly filed in properly labeled folders, so of course, I felt justified to just leave them there.

Please note: Organizing is not the same as decluttering!

Action: Empty 'trash,' delete all 'drafts' older than twelve months, and get rid of all of 'spam' emails.

Subscriptions (newsletters, RSS feeds, etc.)

I have an annoying habit of subscribing to every interesting blog I come across in all social networks in which I am registered. Either I want to see what sort of content they share with their subscribers, or they're offering some cool freebie. But then the notifications arrive, and I ignore them.

The problem with newsletters and notifications is that they'll quickly turn into the virtual equivalent of the cluttered closet if you ignore them.

Remember: Quality over quantity.

Action: Unsubscribe from any newsletter you ignore for more than a month. Schedule a reminder to check what's going on in the blogosphere at least once a week. Assess what you're reading and what you're not, and then make the necessary changes. Make a point of not following all famous blogs at a time, but focus on the quality of the content.

Cloud Storage.

Cloud storage is one area where the digital clutter most appears. Nowadays, we can have Dropbox accounts, Google Drive accounts, and an iCloud account. But still, I see plenty of room here for amalgamation and simplification.

Action: Declutter your own digital space in the cloud storage. Try not to store secondary working files in the cloud storage. Instead, store only what you really need.

There are plenty of opportunities out there for collecting digital clutter. I've included the ones that are most known. But I'm sure there are plenty of others that I haven't thought of. So what about you? How cluttered is your digital life? And what can you do to streamline your cyberspace?

CHAPTER 15:
THE MOST
IMPORTANT
HOURS OF
THE DAY

Perhaps this scenario sounds familiar: you hear the alarm clock go off in the morning, but you just need a couple more minutes of sleep, so you hit the snooze button. Fifteen minutes later, the alarm clock goes off, but you're already sound asleep. Thirty minutes later, you wake up in a panic—you just overslept and are going to be late. You rush out of bed, throw on whatever you can find, and head to the bathroom. You quickly look at your toothbrush and tell yourself there's no time. You gargle, grab whatever is in the fridge for lunch, and you're off.

As you're heading to the door, you notice some invoices on the table, but you don't have time. So you get in your car, hoping there will be no traffic. Finally, you get on the highway, but it's bumper-to-bumper.

Whatever shot you had of having a nice day is gone. The whole way to work, you're thinking up excuses of why you're late today. It becomes one of those days you want entirely to forget.

In the evening, you get home, and any little thing sets you off. You just can't wait for bed!

Your day may not have gone exactly like this, but you've had days that were close, right? So how you spend the first hour of your day will determine how well the rest of it goes. Of course, you can have a bad first hour and turn it around. But nine times out of ten, if you have a bad first hour, the rest of your day is ruined.

So here are four tips for having a great first hour of the day:

1. Get things prepared the night before.

Right before you go to sleep, set yourself up for the next day. Get your clothes ready, and put them in a spot where you can grab them quickly in the morning. (If you have to iron, do it that night.)

Grab everything you'll need in the morning and put it in one spot. So you can wake up and have it ready to go. If you make your own breakfast (and lunch), have it ready in the fridge. Do as much prep work as you can in order to eliminate the hectic morning routine.

2. Get enough sleep.

You have to get a good amount of rest and relax. What that amount is—that's up to you! Your body needs enough sleep for you to function correctly all day. And it's just not natural to not get enough sleep.

3. Get up a little early and have time for yourself.

Wake up at least 10 minutes earlier than usual. That quiet time you spend in the morning, exercising or reading, will calm you and prepare you for the day. The energy after exercising or wisdom after reading you get as a part of that first hour of the morning will be your shield. Even if you can only spare ten minutes, it can go a long way to ensure a positive, stress-free day.

4. Use every minute of the first hour of the day wisely.

During the first hour of the day, you can listen to some soothing music or a podcast that will inspire you. Using every minute of that first hour will help keep you focused throughout the day. If you are intentional with your time, it will lead to amazing results.

At first, you might feel like that those few minutes of sleep are just what your body needs, but that's not true. So make sure you give yourself the proper amount of rest the night before, and when the alarm clock goes off, wake up and hit the ground running. Spend that time wisely and prepare yourself for all the opportunities life will throw at you.

CHAPTER 16: EXAMPLES OF HOW TO SPEND THE FIRST MINUTES OF YOUR DAY WISELY

Many of us spend the first important moments of our days answering emails or listening to voice mail. But a better approach is to begin your day with a brief planning session. Envisioning what you would like to accomplish today separates crucial tasks from those that simply feel urgent.

Next, you need to break down complex tasks into specific actions by starting each item on your to-do list with a verb. Having each step mapped out in advance will minimize complex thinking later in the day (and make procrastination less likely).

Finally, prioritize your list, beginning your day with important tasks that require the most mental energy. Research indicates that we have less willpower as the day progresses. That is why it's best to tackle challenging items early on (particularly those requiring focus and mental agility). Now let's take a closer look at this approach.

The value of applying a mindful approach to work and deliberately taking time out to plan before we begin is very important. What's the first thing you do when you arrive at your office? For many of us, checking email or social media is practically automatic. But in many ways, these are among the worst ways to start a day. Both activities steal our focus and put us in a reactive mode, where other people's priorities take center stage.

So a better approach is to begin your day with a brief planning session. Ask yourself this question the moment you sit at your desk: When the day will over, what I want to achieve?

This simple exercise is usually effective at helping people distinguish between tasks that simply feel urgent from those that are truly important. So use it to determine the activities you want to focus your energy on.

Then—and this is very important—create a plan of action by breaking down complex tasks into specific actions. I recommend starting each item on your list with a verb, which is useful because it makes your intentions concrete. For example, instead of listing "Tuesday's presentation," identify every action item that creating Tuesday's presentation will involve. You may end up with: collect sales figures, draft slides, prepare images and etc.

Modern studies show that the more specific you are about what you're trying to achieve when it comes to goals, the better your chances of success. Also, having each step mapped out in advance will minimize complex thinking later in the day and make procrastination less likely.

Finally, prioritize your plan. When possible, start your day with tasks that require the most mental energy and focus. As mentioned above, research indicates that we have less willpower as the day progresses, which is why it's best to tackle challenging items early on. So that no matter what happens, you will always do only the most essential things first.

The entire exercise can take you less than 5 minutes. And yet, it's a practice that yields significant dividends throughout your day. By starting each day with a mini-planning session, you front-load important decisions to a time when your mind is fresh. You'll also notice that having a list of concrete action items (rather than a broad list of goals) is especially valuable later in the day when fatigue sets in and complex thinking are harder to achieve.

Now, no longer do you have to pause and think through each unnecessary step. Instead, you can devote your full attention to the execution of each important step.

CHAPTER 17: THE 10-MINUTE RULE

The start of a new 2018 year overwhelmed me. Please, do not misunderstand me: I love the idea of shifting gears and walking into a new year. I love the possibility of a new calendar and plans. But I am overwhelmed by all the things I want to do and everything I think I can magically begin, just because January 1 arrives at the front of the calendar.

The new year is tricky because we formulate these big, life-shifting goals, and then we wonder why nothing changes. But why do we quickly shelf those goals and go back to old habits?

I've learned it's because building a new discipline takes time. It is like a muscle we need to train little by little. Progress is usually made out of little things done on repeat.

At the start of 2018, I was feeling worn out before the new year even arrived on the calendar. I had things I wanted to do, but I was drained by the idea of setting another set of lofty resolutions that looked like failures by the middle of January.

So I refocused my approach and decided to zoom in small. I picked one primary goal: Read more books, scroll websites less.

Instead of assuming I had to go out to the bookstore to fill my shelves with new reads that might entice me to create this new habit, I decided to start with what I already had. So I pulled a book off the shelf, and I set a timer on my phone for 10 minutes. Just 10 minutes to read a few pages of a paper book I already had.

A few years removed from that "read more books, scroll websites less" goal, this is how most of my life operates: in 10-minute increments. I call it the "10-minute rule." It's not fancy. It's no fuss. You just set the timer, and you start. Ten minutes to clear your mind and journal. Ten minutes to go for a walk outside. Ten minutes to write some good sentences or call grandparents just to hear their voices.

Most of us have 10 minutes. Often we say we don't, but we could find the space. We could wake up 10 minutes earlier. We could put down our phones. We could watch fewer TV shows. I think we lie to ourselves that we need to have the whole day or a whole hour to invest in something we care about that would make us feel like we will change in the near future. But I'm afraid we'll keep waiting on that miraculous free 12-hour time block or that day off only to find it never shows up.

We'll never find free time in the future. We have to make it today, and we have to decide that even the smallest actions are going to matter. They're going to stack up and contribute to much bigger victories ahead.

On days where I feel overwhelmed by the tasks ahead of me, I set a timer and get to it immediately. I remind myself: you can do anything for 10 minutes.

For example, here is my working tasks range from small to big:

* Appoint a working meeting (5 minutes)

* Go through my inbox (7 minutes)

* Reply to important messages (8 minutes)

* Clean my work desk (10 minutes)

With just 10 minutes, I make progress in a direction that matters to me. So I change the landscape around me and get closer to the goals that really matter to me. It's really all about looking for that tiny thread within infinity tasks and beginning to pull.

Over the years, I've found it doesn't just work for the tasks you are dreading or tasks that need to get done, but it also works even more masterfully for things you've always said you wanted to do. Those things you've quickly pushed to the side with the excuse of, "I just don't have enough time for this."

I've wanted to write a book for years. This idea sat in my mind for so long and haunted me with each passing day. Now I believe in not letting inspiration and ideas sit dormant for too long, so one day I pulled out a notebook I already had and set my timer.

Over the next 10 minutes, I began to do research for the book. I simply used 10 minutes to watch some videos about the writing process and scan through some articles. But there was something about carving out that time that lit energy in me.

It was the first small step in the right direction. I was shocked to see it felt like coming back to myself. I decided I was going to keep writing, ten minutes at a time. The number of minutes seems small, but I'd convince myself there just wasn't enough time.

It needs to happen every single day (except weekends). It's not about getting the 10-minutes down perfectly. It's about deciding to show up and put something that matters at the forefront for just a few moments in your day.

It might take 10 minutes to start cleaning out the closet in your office. You might not finish that big task today, but you're a little bit closer than you where you were before you set the timer.

It might take 10 minutes to write 200 words. But that's 200 more words than you had yesterday.

It might take 10 minutes to research some new recipes. But that's an arsenal of family meals that didn't exist this morning.

If you feel like life has been knocked out of you, or you don't know how to start a new hobby, it may be time to look around the readjust. You don't need to add more hard tasks to your already full life. You don't need to make big money investments or buy fancy gadgets to make progress. You just need to clear the space, maybe just for 10 minutes. You just need to start right where you are and with what you already have.

CHAPTER 18: HELPFUL IDEAS TO DECLUTTER WORKPLACE EVEN ON A BUSY SCHEDULE

People live busy lives sometimes by choice, sometimes by circumstance. Nevertheless, it is a reality of the world we all live in. As a result, there are many who wish to declutter their workplaces but can't find the margin to do so. If that's you, this chapter is for you.

As you declutter, you will almost magically find more free time in your schedule. This is because most of our items are distractions that grab our time and energy. So as you move through work-in spaces, removing things you no longer need, you'll be surprised how quickly time seems to come back to you.

Your decluttering effort is an investment. Time spent decluttering possessions is never wasted. Each person needs to make simplicity a priority in their workspace. Clutter won't remove itself. We need to find the time to push through the initial investment that is required to accomplish this in our homes, jobs, and lives.

There is an oft-cited proverb that goes like this:

> "A person being too busy is a myth. People will always make time for the things that are really important to them."

There is truth in that old statement. Any busy person who wants to declutter their workplace must be willing to make it a priority. How then can we find the time to experience these benefits?

Here are 4 ways to declutter workspace even on a busy schedule:

1. Wake up early or stay up late.

When I first started decluttering my workspace,

there was a three-day stretch when I woke up every morning at 5 am, accomplishing 45 minutes of decluttering before my working day even started. I didn't necessarily need to get up early. But I knew that decluttered workspace inspires new ideas. (If you are more of a night person, choosing to stay after work for a short period of time is also an option.)

2. Turn off the internet on your phone.

Reclaim control over your work by choosing to set aside your electronic device for just 45 minutes/day. Again, this doesn't need to be a permanent change. But for a period of time, it can provide the extra time needed to declutter your workplace even on a busy schedule.

3. Make it "team-time."

One reason finding time to decluttering our possessions can be difficult is because we are shy of our colleagues. But rather than seeing the decluttering of a workplace as isolating yourself, bring them along and do it together. Of course, this may be easier said than done. But don't you think these are important skills you want to share with your colleagues?

4. Make decluttering your hobby.

Hobbies are very important. They educate us, energize us, and provide a valuable space that allows us to re-engage our responsibilities with a fresh mind and body. Make decluttering your hobby. This does not mean you have to give up another hobby, like: reading, painting, gardening, golfing, baking, or woodworking forever. It simply means you are postponing that hobby briefly to craft new opportunities where you can enjoy them more in the future.

Decluttering your workplace is not an easy change to make. For example, suppose you've been accumulating possessions at your job for the last several decades. In that case, it's going to take more than one morning to remove them. But as you progress, you will find caring for your workplace becomes much easier and less time-consuming—resulting in more space in your schedule.

CHAPTER 19: EIGHT 10-MINUTE DECLUTTERING OFFICE PROJECTS

Picture your dream job. I think it's not filled with clutter. Uncluttered spaces are life-giving and promote calm, peace, freedom. But sometimes, uncluttered spaces are challenging to realize. For any number of reasons, workplaces fill up with more and more things. And existing clutter attracts more clutter. As a result, imagining decluttered spaces in our workplaces becomes more and more difficult.

Minimizing all the clutter in our workplaces throughout 10 minutes is not reasonable for most people. However, taking a few small steps in the right direction is possible even for this short time.

Here are eight 10-minute decluttering office projects you can accomplish today:

1. Clean out your car/vehicle.

Too often, our vehicles fill up with unnecessary things: old CDs, sunglasses, receipts, coins, empty water bottles, paper trash. So grab two bags: one for garbage and one for items to relocate. Then, fill them quickly with everything in your car that doesn't need to be there. After 10 minutes, you'll be surprised how quickly you can empty your vehicle of unneeded clutter.

2. Go through the office wardrobe.

To some people, the idea of going through their office wardrobe is overwhelming. But what if you took 10 minutes and just went through it? Start with a wardrobe section that will be fairly easy to make decisions on. Then take all the clothes out of the wardrobe and put them with like-kind. Let go of anything that doesn't fit, you don't like or is in poor condition.

3. Sort through a pile of mail or paper.

Is there a stack of paper files or junk mail on

your office desk? First, look for piles of paper in places they don't belong (office floor, bookshelves, coffee tables) and tackle those piles first. You'll get through them very quickly and easily. Then, if you're feeling motivated, move on to tackle a larger pile—sometimes, taking the first step is the hardest.

4. Clean out medicine chest.

If empty containers, expired products, and dozens of items no longer used are cluttering up your medicine chest, take a few minutes and remove everything that can go.

5. Declutter your plates or cups cupboard.

Many modern offices are filled with duplicate items. Realistically, how many cups, mugs, and plates does your team need? Maybe you have slowly accumulated an entire cupboard full of them? Reach in the back, grab those that are never used, and minimize them forever from valuable office space.

6. Declutter the dining area.

Many offices have kitchen tables that do double duty. Sometimes they are used for projects as well as enjoying meals. Unfortunately, if you have a multi-use table, chances are it tends to attract clutter.

Remove all items that don't belong dining area. Then sort the papers and throw out the trash. Once the table is decluttered, it's so much easier to wipe it down and eat on.

7. Declutter Your PC.

In the perfect office, computers would always be fast, your files and folders would stay organized, and your productivity would never drop. But, unfortunately, things don't work out that way. Just like cars, computers need regular clean-up and maintenance to stay fast. But let's face it—nobody really has the time to perform computer clean-up regularly because there's a misconception that it takes too much time. Although in fact, you can declutter your computer in less than 10 minutes:

Step 1: Close All Running Apps

Step 2: Uninstall Unused Software

Step 3: Clean Out Duplicate Photos, Songs, Videos, and Documents

Step 4: Perform Disk Cleanup

Remember to declutter your PC regularly, and it will stay organized and fast.

8. Create a weekly routine.

Some people find that putting 10 minutes aside at

the end of the workday to tidy up their desks is a great way to maintain a decluttered state. If it works for you, try to build it into a routine so it becomes a routine (it can be just one time a week). It'll prevent clutter from sneaking back in too quickly and set you off to a good start the following week.

I realize, of course, everyone's working places look a little bit different than others. Specifically, for you, one of the projects listed above may take longer than ten minutes. But for the most part, they can be completed very easily and quickly. And whether you accomplish one or all seven, you'll be thankful you did it. Maybe they might not solve all your clutter issues. But they'll definitely get you moving in the right direction. Happy office decluttering!

CHAPTER 20:
DO IT BEFORE
YOU LEAVE
WORK TODAY

My father once gave me one priceless piece of advice. And I have tried to stay true to his advice whenever possible.

"Just clear your desk in the evening, and you'll be thankful in the morning."

A new day brings new opportunities and the potential to accomplish something great. But walking into an office with yesterday's work still visible can immediately anchor you to the past, tying yesterday's rope to today's potential. Instead, a clean desk breeds life, encouragement, and endless possibilities. Even if your new day is going to consist of completing yesterday's project, starting again or re-opening the file offers new opportunities and a new way to see a problem or accomplish a task.

At my work, this Friday has been designated as office clean-up day, complete with turning off phones and minimal office hours. I am very excited because my workspace has become overrun with clutter over the last week. I have done minimal clean-up (mostly desktops) and am looking forward to an entire office make-over.

I have several ideas that I am looking forward to incorporating on Friday, including:

* Remove unnecessary items from my desktop (stackable files, stapler, etc.);

* Sort and store all digital media (CD's, DVD's, and USB drives);

* Transfer old paper files to digital files;

* Take home every book that I have not used or eliminate at least one entire bookshelf;

* Remove some items from walls, including some certificates;

* Remove clutter in my office (sport and travel souvenirs);

* Add a fresh coat of paint—something light, neutral, and less distracting.

You may ask: Is it realistic to clear off your desk EVERY day? Probably not. But I bet you can do it this working day! So do yourself a favor—before you leave work today, clear off your desk. Then, you'll be thankful tomorrow.

CHAPTER 21: HOW TO INTEGRATE MINDFULNESS INTO YOUR WORKDAY

You wake up to the blare of your alarm, rush through or skip breakfast, and get on the bus to head to work. Or maybe you have a car, and on your commute, you might deal with traffic jams and struggle to find a place to park near your office.

Once you finally make it to work, you're met with a hectic meeting schedule, endless unanswered emails, and constant notifications from your various social media channels. You're exhausted and feeling frantic—but the day has barely begun.

Integrating mindfulness into your work can help you stay grounded through the demands of your workday. It can help you find the right balance, decrease stress, and even increase satisfaction and happiness in life.

So let's take a look at a few ways to integrate mindfulness into your workday:

Bell of Mindfulness

Using a bell of mindfulness is an excellent technique for reminding yourself to stay mindful throughout the day. You can use a physical bell, timer, or an alarm on your smartphone (there are also many special free apps). So set your bell or alarm to ring at regular intervals throughout the day. And every time your bell rings, take a few moments to stop doing and just be. Put down whatever it is that you're working on, close your eyes for a moment, and take a few deep, slow breaths.

Each time your bell rings, you have an opportunity to slow down, check-in with yourself, and put things in perspective. The bell of mindfulness can be very grounding, especially in an office environment where you can easily get wrapped up in a million things you're trying to do at once and forget to center yourself.

Mindful Walking

Movement is perhaps one of the most enjoyable and essential ways you can incorporate mindfulness into your workday. If you, like many people, sit at a desk in front of a computer for upwards of eight-nine hours a day, your mental and physical health and well-being are at risk. Sitting for a prolonged period of time impacts vein health, including stress levels, back health, and eye health (just to name a few).

But you can check off the movement and mindfulness boxes on your to-do list by going outside for a short walk whenever you can. Even if you stand up and take a lap around your office once every few hours, you'll give your body a chance to stretch and your mind a chance to recenter and breathe.

Mindful Eating

Eating mindfully can be really challenging to do, especially when you're feeling stressed out or overwhelmed. Eating too quickly or eating while doing something else are all examples of unmindful eating.

Many people who practice mindful eating find that they can transform stress when they stop trying to do several things at once and instead focus solely on one activity at a time (in our case, this is the process of eating). So when lunchtime rolls around, but you're tempted to just eat at your desk and work through your break—think again. You'll likely be more productive and happier if you take 20-30 minutes to enjoy your food away from your desk and focus on eating mindfully.

Grounding Practices

Integrating grounding practices into your daily routines, both when you're at work and when you're at home, can go a long way in making mindfulness a more central part of your life. Spending a portion of each day unplugged from all your devices is a great way to ground yourself and just be present.

One of the great grounding practices is to work in a garden and get your hands dirty. What could be more grounding than literally working with the ground to create natural food or beautiful flowers? The value of community gardens is great, showing the benefits of working with other people in your grounding and mindful practices. After all, one of the most important parts of mindfulness is getting to share it with others.

Mindfulness probably isn't something that is going to just happen to you without any kind of effort. Especially in a world like the one we live in today, mindfulness must be intentionally cultivated and practiced. This means you have to do it repeatedly before you realize you're going through your day in a more mindful way without even thinking about it.

The world might be a different place if most people practiced a few of these mindfulness hacks throughout their days. We often don't realize how stressed and overwhelmed we are until we take a minute to stop, slow down and relax.

The next time you feel stressed out, overwhelmed, and out of touch, use the bell of mindfulness, mindful eating practices, fresh air and movement, and grounding practices. You'll likely feel better and be on your way to developing habits that will be beneficial for the whole world.

CHAPTER 22:
TRAIN YOURSELF
FOR SINGLE-
TASKING

You may think you are a good multi-tasker. But science is showing that even if you are better at it than average, multi-taskers are more likely to be stressed than their single-tasking friends. Besides, none of us are actually very good at multi-tasking because our brains are not designed to do more than one thing at a time.

Stress is hard on the body and leads to digestive problems, heart disease, sleep disruption, and worse memory. It also leads to focus impairment because getting into the zone to complete an important project at work (or at home) takes time. As a result, doing two things at once or rapidly jumping between projects decreases your performance at both.

Meanwhile, the benefits of single-tasking are abundant—from better mood and health to better focus and productivity. And while we may know the benefits of single-tasking, putting it into practice can be challenging. So single-tasking is something we must train ourselves to do—especially in a world intentionally designed to grab our attention and distract us.

Here's how to train yourself for single-tasking:

1. Prioritize.

Every evening or morning, choose the most important tasks you need to complete that day. Start with your most important projects, and work from there.

2. Start with small tasks.

Just like a sportsman would train themselves with manageable exercises first, begin with easier rather than daunting tasks.

3. Break down large projects into smaller chunks.

Build a plan for achieving big goals with less stress. This helps us keep the completion point in sight. It is also a good practice for preventing procrastination.

4. Have only the tools you need for the task available.

Clear your work desk. Close out unimportant computer tabs. Turn off the internet on your phone. You are ready.

5. Take breaks from work.

Work in bursts and setting a timer if necessary. Then slowly increasing the blocks of time in which you'll single-task. And don't forget to take breaks for mental recovery in between.

6. Enjoy the sensation of completing the time or the task.

Notice your gratitude as you cross another item off the to-do list. Then use that sense of accomplishment to carry you forward.

7. Remember that sometimes the goal isn't perfection—it's progress.

Don't expect to be perfect the first time you try (or even after many attempts). The goal of single-tasking is to get better, not to get perfect.

If you train yourself to make single-tasking an ingrained habit in your work, you'll begin accom-

plishing your goals much faster than you antici-
pate. And over time, this approach will also spread
into your daily life.

CHAPTER 23: KEEPING A JOURNAL CAN HELP YOU REACH YOUR GOALS

Many people are often interested in learning how to journal. But they're unsure how keeping a journal can help them with their goals.

"Always carry a notebook. And I mean always. The short-term memory only retains information for three minutes; unless it is committed to paper, you can lose an idea forever." — Will Self

I use the discipline of keeping a journal, and it assists me in the pursuit of my work and life goals as well. And I have come to clearly recognize its importance.

Consider these 7 Benefits of Keeping a Journal:

* Keeping a journal requires us to write out our goals.

The importance of committing our goals to paper cannot be overstated. It is a very simple process, but it pays great dividends. Writing out our goals provides us the opportunity to articulate them clearly and makes their achievement appear closer.

* Even a private journal provides responsibility.

As we script our journey, we find responsibility—not to the written word, but to ourselves. Our past perseverance compels us forward. We can clearly see how far we've come, how much we have left to accomplish, and why giving up would be foolish.

* Writing goals requires us to think through the why's and the how's.

When we sit down behind a blank computer screen or sheet of paper and begin to write out what we accomplished during the day, we are forced to think through our process on a much deeper level. The discipline of journaling forces us to answer the difficult questions of "why," "how," or "why not?" The answers to these questions are not just helpful as we move forward to repeat successes and avoid mistakes—they can be therapeutic as well.

* A journal proves we have solved problems in the past.

Whether we are chasing a career goal or a life goal, not every step in our pursuit is going to be easy. At some point, we will be required to overcome difficulties. But we can. And the next time we face it, we'll find motivation and strength in our written records of overcoming it in the past.

* A journal serves as a permanent record of our progress.

Every success can be quickly forgotten. And when it is, it becomes easy to get frustrated with our work. As with any work, there are times we may feel like we have not accomplished anything despite all the invested effort and energy. So during those moments, it is helpful to look back and be reminded of our past successes.

* Keeping a journal naturally reminds us to articulate the next steps.

It isn't easy to look back without also looking forward. As a result, when we journal, we naturally begin to look forward to the near future. And the next steps become easier to see.

* A written account allows our story to inspire others.

Our journal is our private story. It is our journey of moving from Point A to Point B. But rightly shared, it can inspire others to do the same.

So, how to journal successfully? Here are my recommendations:

1. Find a form that is comfortable for you.

For the beginning, learning how to start journaling is simple, and choose the method you're comfortable with. A personal journal should work for you —not the other way around. You may feel most comfortable with a laptop or an online writing app. Find a form that best fits your personality and lifestyle and embrace it.

2. Commit to writing every day.

The intention of sitting to write every day will compel your mind to manufacture and recognize your progress. Of course, you'll likely miss days. But don't let that stop you! Commit again to write again.

3. Don't be motivated by length.

There are some days where you'll be motivated to write quickly and much. Other days slow and little. But that's the way it should be.

4. Care more about substance and less about style.

Write for yourself, not for other people. As you do, write with the most actual goal and putting onto paper your thoughts and action. And don't worry about spelling and grammar if those things tend to bog you down. Your primary goal is not to get an "A." Your primary goal is to articulate progress.

5. Share your achievements.

Your story may be unique to you, but some people desperately need to know it. So share your best experiences with people who really need them.

I think, after reading this chapter, it is the best time for you to start journaling. So put the book aside for a time and get started.

CHAPTER 24: ACCOMPLISH MORE WITH A 3-ITEM TO-DO LIST

For many years, I was the person with a mile-long to-do list, often carrying over from day-to-day and week-to-week. But no longer! Now I use the 3-Item To-Do List. And I'd love to recommend it to you.

For the past several months, I have been using a 3-Item To-Do List exclusively. And I have found it to increase my productivity and work satisfaction significantly.

The 3-Item To-Do List is as simple and profound as it sounds. At the beginning of each day, I take a few minutes to identify and articulate the three most important items for me to accomplish.

For example, my 3-Item To-Do List for today consists of these three items:

1. Write 1 500 words for my new book.

2. Carry out an analysis of financial expenses for advertising for the previous month.

3. Analyze the article on keyword research.

That's it! Three items—all important, all significant, and all entirely manageable. Now, almost certainly, there are other work-related things I will do today. But my three main identified tasks will always take precedence.

The shortlist approach keeps me focused on the most important tasks I need to accomplish. But I also have found other benefits as well. For example, the shorter list keeps me from feeling overwhelmed. And the shorter list also helps me overcome procrastination—the finish line is always in sight.

Additionally, and equally important, the 3-Item To-Do List provides a sense of accomplishment at the end of each day. When the to-do list is completed, there is a sense of finality.

The importance of identifying the three most important tasks to accomplish in a day is revolutionary regardless of where you apply it. It is a helpful productivity hack at any work. It can be uniquely tailored for a hobby or side business. It also can be used equally well by a stay-at-home parent.

So in order to accomplish our most important tasks, it is essential to remain focused on them. The 3-Item To-Do List helps with that and requires you to identify them anew each day.

CHAPTER 25:
WHY YOUR SELF-WORTH IS MORE IMPORTANT THAN YOUR NET-WORTH

As humans, it is in our nature to compare ourselves to other people. Unfortunately, because we can only compare the things that we can objectively measure, we live in a world that is great at measuring and comparing only externals. Somewhere along the way, we decided that we could determine who is living a more valuable life by comparing their clothes, homes, cars, and net-worth.

*Net-worth: Your assets minus your debts.

*Self-worth: The quality of being worthy of esteem and respect.

Simply put, we tied our self-worth to net worth. As a result, we began to make judgments about our own life values by the possessions that we own. But, in reality, our life is far more valuable than the physical things that we own.

Of course, the wages that we earn provide for our lives—but they do not define our lives. Fortunately, when we change our thinking on this matter, we are freed to pursue a life worthy of esteem and respect that is not tied only to our possessions.

> *"There is no value in life except what you choose to place upon it and no happiness in any place except what you bring to it yourself." — Henry David Thoreau*

So, consider these 8 steps to improve your self-worth regardless of your net-worth:

1. Accept your weaknesses.

There are no perfect people in this big world. We all have some struggles and weaknesses. However, I have found that one of the best ways to identify with others is in our weaknesses. Because when we admit that we need help, we are finally ready to interact with others on a truly valuable level.

2. Delight in your uniqueness.

The simple fact that you are different from everybody else makes you valuable. So be comfortable with yourself and proud of yourself. Don't suppress yourself. Instead, do the opposite: Save your uniqueness.

3. Live a life without regrets.

There is no more excellent feeling than laying your head on your pillow at night having no regrets in your dealings with others. Consider the immeasurable values that come from looking back over your entire life and seeing the same thing.

4. Live courageously.

Find the mental strength to accept new challenges without regard to the fear that may lie beneath. Live with great expectations about what your life can become and accomplish today.

5. Develop self-confidence.

A confident person feels better about themselves and smiles more. A confident person does not follow the crowd or try to become someone else. Instead, a confident person focuses on their achievements and anticipates their next opportunity in life with excitement. And the good news is: There's always time to learn how to be more confident.

6. Cultivate worthy endeavors that are available in infinite supply.

There is no limit to the amount of respect you can show, the amount of hope you can spread, or the number of encouraging words you can speak. Cultivate these things every day. They will cost you nothing but will begin to mean everything.

7. Share your most valuable resources.

The most precious resources we own are our time and energy. Therefore, the most precious things that we can ever give to another person are our time and energy. So make a habit of giving it away to others.

8. Make the most of every opportunity.

Each new day brings with it new opportunities, so don't waste a single one. Instead, do everything you do with quality, excellence, and joy.

It's time to realize that your true self-worth is up to you. So don't allow your life's pursuit to be caught up in the acquisition of material things that makes for a high net-worth, but not necessarily high self-worth. Your self-worth must trump your net-worth.

CHAPTER 26: MAIN FACTORS TO LOOK FOR IN A NEW JOB OTHER THAN A PAYCHECK

Have you ever been asked, "What do you look for?" Perhaps a colleague has asked you that out of curiosity, or you've heard it at a job interview. Unfortunately, the default thought is often the pay. After all, that's why many of us get jobs. But dig deeper, and you will find many more factors to consider in what to look for in a job.

Decluttering has many benefits. It gives freedom, time and reduces stress. Decluttering also reduces the amount of money required for life. As a result, it provides an opportunity to choose work based on many factors—not just the size of the paycheck.

Once we learn contentment with free space, we are free to weigh any number of factors in choosing work. Embrace the 5 Steps Method. It opens up countless opportunities in life and work.

"Never continue in a job you don't enjoy. If you're happy with what you're doing, you'll like yourself, you'll have inner peace. And if you have that, along with physical health, you'll have more success than you could possibly have imagined." — Roger Caras

To help you enjoy waking up in the morning, consider these 12 things to look for in a new job:

1. It fits your personality

Anyone who has ever taken a personality test knows we all have unique personalities that thrive in specific environments. Some enjoy working with people, while others enjoy completing tasks. Some people like making the decisions, while others don't. So find a job that fits your sweet spot.

2. It is something you love to do

If you find a job that you love—you'll never have to work a day in your life. So look for a job that keeps you motivated by its very nature, not solely by the paycheck, because that wears off real fast.

3. It brings balance to life

Hard work is not so bad when you love it. But if you are not allowed to explore other endeavors (play, hobbies, and family) because of its demands, it is not healthy for your life. So find a job that allows you to enjoy your life outside of work too.

4. The company's values align with yours

At the end of the workday, your integrity is what matters most. So don't compromise it every time you walk into the workplace. If you are at a job that requires you to suspend your personal convictions —you shouldn't need to stay.

5. It values family

You value your family, and your job should too.

6. A flexible, results-oriented culture

A culture of flexibility suggests a results-driven focus. This one is more interested in you successfully completing your job with excellence than clocking in a set amount of work hours.

7. It challenges you to grow

Look for a job that will make you better as a professional and allow you to work hard. Whether through educational opportunities, challenging assignments, demanding excellence, or informal mentors, a job that forces you to grow beyond your current skill set will make you a better person (and make the company you work in better too).

8. It makes a positive difference

Choose a job that adds value to our world, leaves it better than you found it, and genuinely helps other people live better.

9. You feel appreciated and valued

A paycheck is nice, but that goes straight to the bank account. On the other hand, appreciation is something you carry in your heart every day. This appreciation can be communicated through respect, unexpected bonuses, or just an old-fashioned "thank-you."

10. You enjoy your co-workers

Given the fact that you will spend a large percentage of your day at work, be sure you enjoy the people you work with. It is comforting to know that they support you and work together as a team.

11. You are trusted

It's nice to know that somebody isn't always looking over your shoulders. And when you are given a task, you are given the freedom to complete it yourself.

12. It brings you satisfaction

The ability to look back at your day, year, or life with satisfaction is more valuable than any number of digits in the bank account. Do work you love!

Next time you're asked about what you're looking for in your job, you'll have a dozen great answers that go beyond just pay.

CHAPTER 27:
BETTER FILTERS

When deciding to make a financial purchase or not, the most common filter we ask ourselves is, "Can I afford it?" But "Can I afford it?" is a terrible filter. Is there enough money in the bank or room on the credit card to cover this purchase? If so, we can easily buy it.

From home we live in, the clothes we wear, the car we drive, the vacations we take, the technology we upgrade, and everything in-between, most people simply ask, "Can I afford it?" I've seen this kind of thinking in my own life. No doubt, you have experienced this thought as well.

Often times it is coupled with an "I deserve it" mentality. As in, "I work hard, and I am going to spend my money on this because I deserve it, and I can afford it."

But here's the issue: "Can I afford it?" is actually a

terrible filter for making financial decisions! Or, let me rephrase that "Can I afford it?" is a terrible filter if it is the only filter we use in making decisions about what to buy and how to spend our money. It's not wrong in and of itself. It's just incomplete. Unfortunately, for many of us, it is the only filter.

We think if the money is in the bank account, we can buy anything we desire. Why not? We can afford it. But consider some of the main reasons why it's a terrible filter:

It Doesn't Count the Full Cost of Our Purchase.

The amount listed on a price tag is never the total cost of a purchase. Everything we purchase needs to be brought home and eventually maintained, organized and cared for. Everything we buy takes up physical space in our home and mental space in our minds.

Many of our purchases also result in extra expenditures, whether directly or indirectly. "Do I have enough money, right now, to afford this item?" rarely factors in the ongoing cost of keeping or maintaining our purchase.

Financial Count That Circumstances Change All the Time.

One lesson I hope we've all noticed is that financial

circumstances can change in a heartbeat and almost without warning. If your decision to buy a car at the very top of your price range or take out a new house loan was based solely on "Can I afford it?" you may be surprised how quickly that can change.

It Doesn't Count Opportunity Cost.

Spending $100 on X today means you do not have $100 to spend on Y tomorrow. This is why "Can I afford it?" is such a short-sighted filter.

You may have the money to buy a bigger house, a more excellent vacation, or a newer car. Still, once the purchase is completed, that money is no longer available for other things. And it may not take long to realize there were countless other things you could have spent your money on that would have resulted in much longer-lasting joy, happiness, and fulfillment.

So what questions can you ask yourself in addition to "Can I afford it?" Let me offer some of the most important:

1. What are my motivations for this purchase?

Am I spending my money on this purchase for the right reason? What is it exactly? Am I buying this just because everyone else is buying it because I'm trying to impress someone? Or are my motivations truly healthy?

2. Does this purchase support my goals?

What are the most valuable dreams you have for your life? What accomplishments are you hoping to achieve in the near future? What goals are most important to you and your relatives? Does this purchase move you closer to your goals? Or, instead, further away?

3. Is there something else I would like to spend my money on?

When counting the opportunity cost of your purchase, don't compare only apples to apples. The filter doesn't need to be exclusive, "Should I buy this car or this home?"

We should also factor in opportunities such as getting out of debt, getting ahead financially, and giving to a cause we believe in. Spending money on purchasing "just because I can afford it" often makes these more significant pursuits harder to achieve.

4. What would my life look like if I said no?

We often find ourselves debating a purchase because we've considered what benefits the purchase will bring into our lives. But rarely do we take the time to honestly evaluate what benefits might arise if we said "no."

With every purchase, we sacrifice a small amount of freedom. This one simple filter helps us recognize what that is exactly.

5. What do my trusted people think about this?

There is no need to make financial decisions in a vacuum (especially major ones). Ask a family member or friend, or mentor for their opinion. Make sure it is someone you trust.

Before I conclude, let me be clear on the two most important points:

First, sometimes it is wise to ask ourselves, "Can I afford it?" I mean, if you can't afford it, you shouldn't buy it, and the case is closed.

Second, this point of view isn't contending that we never make any purchase. That would not be very smart. To live is to consume, and many of the investments we make do bring value to our lives.

So this list of most significant filters isn't meant to deter anyone from ever spending money again. Instead, it's simply designed to help people make better choices.

CHAPTER 28:
A PERSONAL
SPENDING PLAN
THAT ACTUALLY
WORKS

We all know the importance of having a personal budget and holding to it. But discipline is sometimes not a priority in our lives.

> *"We must consult our means rather than our wishes." — George Washington*

But everything can change when we realize the idea of creating a "spending plan" rather than a "budget." As for me, I have used this spending plan system with great pleasure over the past several years after being introduced to it.

The idea that distinguishes this specific spending plan from a typical budget is the understanding that while a budget dictates to you what, where, and when you can spend, a spending plan allows you to be aware of your needs. Also, it realizes that your purchases change and expenses vary from month to month and that a one-size-fits-all monthly budget doesn't truly fit anymore.

Using the spending plan model is quite simple! Although it does require some effort on the front end and throughout the month (just like any personal financial system). So, let's begin:

Step 1. To get started, determine your monthly take-home pay (not your gross income before taxes, but your net income—the actual amount on your check or direct deposit):

NET INCOME IN JANUARY—xxx$

Step 2. Second, sit down and determine all your fixed monthly costs. These are the expenses you currently have in your life that require some of your income every single month—no questions asked. The actual monthly expense may vary from month to month, but you know it is going to be there. For example:

* Mortgage—xxx$

* Health Insurance—xxx$

* Utilities: Gas, Electricity, Water, Garbage—xxx$

* Home Internet—xxx$

* Cell phone—xxx$

* Auto insurance—xxx$

* Auto Fuel/Maintenance—xxx$

* Kids' School/Activities—xxx$

* College loan repayment—xxx$

TOTAL FIXED MONTHLY COSTS IN JANUARY—xxx $

Step 3. After determining your monthly income and monthly fixed costs, you can easily recognize your monthly discretionary income (the money you have left over spending as you desire). Just subtract your monthly fixed costs (Step 2) from your monthly net income (Step 1). For example, if you have $1000 per month left over after paying your fixed costs, you have $1000 in discretionary income. The spending plan now allows you the opportunity to spend that $1000 as you desire: food, entertainment, devices, travel, or extra savings. The choice is yours!

Note: Discretionary income is the amount of an individual's income that is left for spending, investing, or saving after paying taxes and paying for personal necessities, such as food, clothing, and shelter.

I have found wonderful benefits to this personal spending plan:

1. The personal spending plan does not require meticulous tracking. Most of our costs are fixed. They do not vary much from month to month. Rather than having to track individual expenses each day of the month, we are primarily concerned with only tracking the amount of our discretionary income spent and remaining for the month.

2. The personal spending plan helps sort needs from wants as our fixed costs are initially calculated. And we begin to quickly realize which expenses are truly fixed and which are not.

3. The initial realization of your discretionary income gives a real opportunity to determine how much money you actually have to spend each month.

4. The plan allows you to see how financial patterns affect your life. For example, if you lay out your plan and realize that you need more discretionary income, you have a list of fixed costs that could possibly be reduced.

5. You will be able to easily recognize how country economics should be influencing your spending.
For example, if auto fuel goes up $0.5/gallon, you can quickly recalculate your fixed costs and determine how much discretionary income has taken a hit. Conversely, if fuel goes down $0.5/gallon, you'll have a little extra that you can spend or save that month.

Even if you don't hold yourself to consistent tracking of expenses throughout each month, I do recommend going through the personal spending plan just to get a sense of your "actual discretionary income." It can probably be completed in less than 20 minutes. And it will result in new discoveries about the state of your personal finances. It may also be the right first step in finally finding a spending plan for your household that actually works.

CHAPTER 29: A PRACTICAL SOLUTION TO ALMOST ALL YOUR MONEY PROBLEMS

A lmost each of us has money problems. In fact, we always live with a deep sense of personal discontent (or unease) concerning our use of money. This discontent concerning our finances came from two areas:

First, we are too often discontent with the amount of money we spend. We often live paycheck-to-paycheck. And even despite ever-increasing paychecks, we are never able to build up any substantial savings. Our credit card bill seemed to mimic our pay stub. The money came in, and the money went out.

Second, we are too often discontent with where our money is being spent. Unfortunately, our bank accounts never align with our stated beliefs. We all have an inner desire to care for the poor, but often, we justify ourselves by our financial insolvency when it comes to a real case to help.

In both regards, a solution seems very simple—to get rid of over spending. In simple words, the best solution is to buy less.

Just to be clear, the resolution of buying less is not a new solution. But maybe this solution just had never sounded attractive to you before? Buying less sounds like you need to take a step backward in life, admit defeat, and be unable to earn the income necessary to live according to your dream. It sounds boring, unfashionable, and destined for ridicule. But this is a misconception.

"Go out in the world and work like money doesn't matter, sing as if no one is listening, love as if you have never been hurt, and dance as if no one is watching." — Victor Hugo.

Deciding to intentionally buy less is among the best decisions you can make in your life. As a result of determining to only buy things that are needed, we can find life greatly improved.

We find more opportunities to pursue the greatest passions in our lives.

We discover more time, energy, space, and money available to us than ever before.

We spend less time cleaning, organizing, and repairing the unuseful stuff in our lives.

And rather than chasing every new product or fashion line sold at the department store, we are finally able to invest in the things that make our lives worthwhile.

In this simple solution of buying less, both avenues of financial discontent in our lives (that mentioned above) have been resolved. So for our financial discontent, the practical solution of buying less is perfect.

But what about other financial problems? Would the mindful practice of intentionally buying less easily solve them too? In most cases, it would!

Now, let's consider some of the most all-too-common money problems and how their solution is found in simply buying less:

Deep in debt.

According to CNN, the average American household carries nearly $10,700 in credit card debt. Buying less provides the opportunity to begin repaying that debt slowly but steadily. Of course, ys, it takes time. But persistence, patience, and discipline will absolutely free you from that crippling financial burden. And if buying too much is the cause of many problems, buying less is most certainly the solution.

Don't make enough money.

More often than not, this money problem springs from an internal desire to purchase luxuries that we believe will add happiness to our lives. Because our income does not match our desires, we think that we aren't making enough money. But happiness from luxury is short-lived and can never really satisfy. Your heart will always desire more, and your income will never match your thirst. Instead, an intentional decision to buy less will provide the inner space to find contentment in your current life and begin making the most of it today.

Work is like a trap.

Some people that I know feel trapped in their present employment. Their internal groaning is often heard in statements like, "Can't wait for my promotion." And while some feel trapped because of their real needs, others feel trapped because they used to live too luxuriously. So if you feel trapped, know that the invitation to "buy less" remains open. The decision to buy less will open the door to surviving on a tighter budget and soon open the door to finding work you love.

Fear of retirement.

The most important key to building retirement savings is to start saving today and contribute consistently. Whether you are 20, 30, or 40, your retirement account will not grow substantially without your contributions. So get started today with this simple formula: Buy less—save more.

The family is falling apart due to financial stress.

It is true that one of the leading causes of divorce today is financial stress. This stress stems from any number of factors: pressure from existing debt, disagreements on spending, and financial secrets. Depending on your specific circumstance, intentionally buying less may not solve all of them quickly. But it certainly can't hurt your family. And maybe the extra financial space created from even one partner deciding to buy less will provide the opportunities to resolve family differences.

Your specific money problem may not have been addressed in the list above. Unfortunately, there is just no opportunity to address every financial condition in this limited chapter. But my primary goal was not to specifically address every possible avenue of financial discontent. Instead, I hoped to raise your personal awareness towards the simple, practical solution that resolved the financial discontent at any circumstance: Buy less.

So whatever financial stress you may be feeling today, know that buying less is probably the most practical solution. And the road to financial stability may, in fact, be far more appealing than you think.

CHAPTER 30:
SOMEONE HAS MORE THAN YOU, SO GET USED TO IT

I once read a fascinating statistic about million-aires who lost their money. A survey was con-ducted of people who once had a net worth of $2 million but now are worth less than $1 million. When asked how they lost half their fortune, 40% responded: "We started hanging out with people worth $10 million, and we lost our money trying to match their spending."

The study reveals an important truth: There is al-ways going to be someone in the world with more than you, and trying to keep up with them is a losing battle because there will always be someone else ahead of you in this game. That is always going to be the case:

* There is a neighbor who has more than you.

* There is a co-worker who has more than you.

* Someone at your community group has more than you.

* There is a family at your kid's school who has more than you.

* And we all know there is someone on television right now who has more than we.

Now, it seems to me there are only a couple of responses we can have to this reality:

1. We accept it and decide to find happiness with what we already have.

2. We get jealous and envious, and bitter that someone has more.

The clear choice for a joyful and happy life is #1.

But too often, we choose #2.

As a result, we spend much of our time comparing our things to other people. For example, we compare the size of our house, the year of our automobile, the brand of our clothing, our last vacation destination, the model of our devices, or our paycheck with the person next to us.

Unfortunately, there is no real happiness to be found in these comparisons because there is always going to be someone with more. Therefore, there is no contentment to be found in comparing our stuff with other people.

You may think that once you own a fancy house or nice car like so-and-so, you'll be happy. But that's simply not the case because there will always be someone else to compare yourself to—always a bigger house, a more prestigious car, or a fancier model device to own. So there is no end to the comparison game. There is always going to be someone in the world with more.

But think about next: If you are reading these words, your needs are met. You have food, clothes, and shelter. You may not have the most expensive clothes in the world, you may not eat at the fanciest restaurants, and you may not live in the biggest house in your city. But your primal needs are being met.

I may take this moment to declare another truth: Not only is there someone in this world with more than you, but there is also someone in this world with less than you. There is someone in this world with less than you who is perfectly content because they have chosen to be happy right where they are, rather than comparing their lives to someone with more.

There is someone in this world with more than you. But you have many reasons to be really grateful. And you have everything you need to find happiness in your life. So stop comparing and be truly rich deeply in your heart.

CHAPTER 31: HOW TO PACK WHEN YOU ARE MOVING TO A NEW PLACE

One thing that stresses people out about moving to a new place is packing. And I used to be one of those people.

I was a really over-packer. And, if the situation ever came up where I had packed everything, and I still had a little space left in my suitcase, I felt like I'd won the lottery. I believe that "more space—more physical things" is the best approach. And I'd run around looking for other things that would fill the empty space. I might need that stuff just in case.

The 5 Steps decluttering method has inspired me to move to a new place with less. Everything I pack fits into a big carry-on suitcase and tote bag. So if you are changing your job and want to move to a new place with a little less baggage, I hope you'll enjoy my best packing tips.

Suppose you got a new job for which you have to move to another city. In this case, I want to share with you the best tips on how to pack when moving to a new place:

Create packing lists.

Before your move, list everything you bring with you. During the week before moving, underline each thing in the list when you use it. Then, at the end of the week, you'll know you can leave anything that wasn't underlined. Keep your list handy with details about where you were and what time of year, and save so the next time you move to another place, you'll know what to pack first.

Create a travel day uniform.

Before packing, assign one outfit for your travel day. Then you don't have to think about how to pack these clothes and what to wear on the train, plane, ship, or however you are traveling.

Experiment with packing methods.

I've tried rolling, stacking, and folding my clothes for packing but haven't noticed a big space difference. Now I roll my bottoms and fold my tops—so I find my clothes end up with fewer wrinkles, and I can fit more in my bag. But the only way to really know what works best for you is to experiment and see which method you prefer.

Remember: Just in a case means never.

When you notice you are adding items to your suitcase just in case, then stop and ask yourself why you need it:

Will you really use it?

Or do you just want to fill the empty space in your suitcase?

What's the worst thing that could happen if you don't pack it?

Don't forget what matters most.

If all of your focus is on your stuff and what to pack, you may miss out on what really matters, like connecting with people on your new job or enjoying new locations. Also, don't forget about your professional qualities and take care of yourself while moving.

Moving is always exciting. New opportunities and acquaintances await you ahead. So don't drag your entire past with you, but make room for something new instead.

CHAPTER 32: HOW TO DECLUTTER WHEN YOU ARE MOVING

There is a joy that remains after every move. Paring down items, packing up, and moving are ongoing growthful processes. Moving empowers us to have a healthier relationship with our possessions.

When we move, we are required to physically handle each of our possessions many times:

Put it in a box — Take it out of the house — Bring it into the new home — Unpack, and put it away.

So it is, unarguably, one of the best times in life to declutter possessions. If you've got a transition coming up or are right in the middle of one now, here are seven ways to declutter when you are moving:

1. Get started early.

Packing up a home (and decluttering along the way) always takes more time than we think. So get started earlier than you think. Moving is an important time to declutter your possessions. Also, getting started early will keep you from the familiar panic as moving day inevitably creeps up on you.

2. Change your perspective to collect and hoard.

Living in space for years allows us to collect and add more things. But moving allows us to challenge these urges and avoid hoarding tendencies. While this might be a hoarder's nightmare, moving forces us to refocus on what we choose to collect today and in the future.

3. Evaluate everything.

The act of picking up, packing, and lifting full boxes can provide an appreciation for what we continue to carry in our lives. As a result, moves prompt us to consider what we've taken for granted. These times allow us to question our choices and our owner-ship. But, to place that item in a box means you'll continue to carry it. So, ask yourself:

Why do I own this?

What does this object provide me?

Am I ready want to continue carrying this?

4. Scan for dust.

Rub your finger along your old items: Does it have dust? This simple trick is something you can use to judge usefulness. Dust can be your friend when you're looking to lighten your suitcase.

5. Ask for advice from family and friends.

Moving always involves great psychological and physical effort. So family and friends can provide incredible help in these times. Surprisingly, close people also help us make important decisions when moving. For example, friends can be quick to ask, "Why do you have three raincoats at the back of the closet?" So they're asking the questions we need to be asking ourselves, as well. Additionally, having help can provide an appreciation and gratitude for those around you.

6. Practice letting go.

It is essential to realize that consumption can never be completely quenched. Marketers will continue to try and sell us more stuff. But there is much freedom to be found in getting rid of unnecessary stuff. And moving provides us a natural reason to practice letting go. We let go of our possessions and our past.

7. Donate or sell stuff.

There are many non-profit organizations where you can donate unnecessary items. Also, the secondhand stores allow you to make a little extra money from all you declutter. So these opportunities keep us grounded and allow for more generous considerations. As a result, we're thinking about others' needs when giving—which has benefits of its own.

Consider looking for ways to engage in decluttering processes whenever you can: Evaluate, ask for advice, let go, donate or sell. And regardless of whether you're moving next week or today, it's never too late to start decluttering.

CHAPTER 33: INTANGIBLE WAYS TO IMPRESS YOUR NEW COLLEAGUES

More often than we would care to admit, the desire to impress others motivates our actions. This desire to impress others impacts the clothes we wear, the technology we embrace, the cars we drive, and the careers we choose. Unfortunately, it is often elusive—cars rust, fashion changes, and technology are progressing. So the purchases that impressed your colleague yesterday make no impression today. As a result, we live our lives with out-of-style clothes, skyrocketing personal debt, hate our jobs, and jealousy towards our colleagues who seems to have it all. Then that unquenchable desire to impress begs us to begin the cycle again.

"The need to impress others causes half the world's woes." — *Vernon Howard*

But the hard truth is we often look to impress others in all the wrong places. Now, take a moment and identify the people in your life that truly impress you. What is it about their life that inspires you most? Make a list if you want. I suggest, very rarely (if ever), it is the car that they drive or the size of their home. Most often, the people who truly inspire us to possess the invisible, intangible qualities that we all desire. But what are these qualities, and how to cultivate them in ourselves?

Consider this list of 15 intangible, surefire ways to impress your new colleagues:

1. Don't live to impress—live to inspire.

Give up your desire to impress everyone you meet at your new workplace. But never give up your inner desire to inspire everyone you meet.

2. Be modest.

You are special and unique. And the less you make an effort to tell everyone that, the more they will notice it.

3. Be content.

A contented life is always enjoyable, desirable, and admirable. Those who don't have it—desire it and are impressed with those who have.

4. Love your life.

Don't fall into the trap of living your life like everyone else. Avoid propaganda. Embrace your passions. Find enjoyment in your life. And the people around you will be impressed.

5. Love your family (and legacy).

And by love your family, I mean genuinely like them too. Enjoy being with members of your family, spending time with them, and investing in their lives. This love towards your relatives will be evident in your life even when they aren't around.

6. Love nature.

People who exhibit care for the nature around us exhibit care for all humanity.

7. Develop your inner strengths.

I am impressed by good CEOs, speakers, singers, authors, writers, architects, computer programmers, and athletes (just to name a few). There is only one thing they all have in common: They discovered their inner strengths and developed them with great discipline. Do the same with your unique giftedness and talents. And regardless of the profession you choose, you will impress.

8. Travel.

See the world around you, and you will change.

9. Listen intently.

Cell phone off. Eyes focused. Ears tuned. In a world that is always in a hurry, someone who can find time to listen is as rare as a precious jewel. And far more valuable.

10. Appreciate different opinions.

While there is nothing wrong with being dogmatic in your beliefs, a healthy appreciation of how your colleagues came to theirs is definitely an impressive quality.

11. Be honest with your colleagues.

Honesty is going out of style too quickly these days.

So stay honest with the team you chose. Trust me—your colleagues will be impressed.

12. Be generous.

Regularly give your attention to others without expecting anything in return. The giving of your attention to another is one of the most impressive things you can ever do.

13. Be optimistic.

Always focus on the good aspects of people and situations. Sometimes you have to focus harder than others, but you'll always be glad you did.

14. Laugh when you want it.

Don't suppress your laughter. Be that person that routinely laughs at other's jokes and funny stories. It concretely communicates that you enjoy their company. Your colleagues will be impressed, and you'll be a more joyful person.

15. Help when it is really needed.

Living your life in competition with your colleagues you will never impress. After all, most people are already doing that. Instead, change the world by being yourself. Seek to help and lift up others. As a result, the person who benefits the most just may be you.

Of course, the most remarkable thing about this list is that you already possess everything you need to inspire others. So why not use it? So stop trying to impress others with the things that you own and begin inspiring them by the way you live your life.

CHAPTER 34: HOW TO STOP COMPARING YOURSELF TO YOUR COLLEAGUES

I've struggled with comparison for a significant part of my life (and maybe I still don't completely get rid of this bad habit). To be truly honest, it is simply a character flaw hidden somewhere deep in my heart.

"Comparison is the thief of joy." — *Theodore Roosevelt*

I often compare myself to others. At first, it was at school. But as I got older, I began comparing other metrics: job title, income level, and general successes.

I have discovered an infinite number of criteria upon which we can compare ourselves and an endless number of people to compare ourselves. With how flooded we are by social media, it's easier than ever to constantly find someone "better" to compare ourselves to, which only makes us feel bad about ourselves. But once we begin down that road, we never find contentment until we turn off this path.

Certainly, I'm not alone in my experience because the tendency to compare ourselves to others is a general human habit. But it is a decision that only steals happiness from our lives.

Comparison is a habit with numerous shortcomings:

* Comparisons rob us of precious time and energy. Each of us gets 1440 minutes each day. And using even one minute to compare yourself to others is one minute too many.

* Comparisons, by definition, require metrics. But not every good thing can be counted or measured.

* There is no end to the possible number of com-

parisons in your life. This habit can never be overcome by attaining success. There always will be someone else for comparison in the future.

* Comparison always puts focus on the other person. But you can control only one life—yours. As a result, when we constantly compare ourselves to others, we waste precious energy focusing on other peoples' lives rather than our own.

* Comparisons are always unfair. We typically compare the worst we know of ourselves to the best we presume about other people.

* We are too unique to compare fairly. Our gifts and talents and successes and contributions and values are entirely unique to us and our purpose in this world. So they can never be properly compared to anyone else.

* Comparisons often result in resentment in our lives. This is resentment towards others and ourselves.

* Comparisons deprive us of happiness. They add no meaning or value to our lives. On the contrary, comparisons only distract from it.

Indeed, the negative effects of comparisons are broad and far-reaching. Possibly, you are experiencing (or have experienced) many of them first-hand in your life as well. How then might we break free from this habit of comparison? How do we stop constantly comparing ourselves to others?

Here are 9 useful tips on how to stop comparing yourself to your colleagues:

1. Be aware of its harmful effects.

Take notice of the negative effects of comparing yourself to others. Then, intentionally remove it from the inside-out to free yourself from the damage this mindset has had on you.

2. Take a walk.

The next moment you find yourself comparing yourself to others, get up, and change your surroundings. For example, go for a walk—even if only to the other side of the office. Allow the change in your surroundings to prompt a change in your thinking.

3. Find inspiration without comparison.

If the comparison is a consistent tendency in your life, notice which attitudes prompt positive change and which result in negative influence. Then find inspiration and learn from others—it is entirely wise. Humbly ask questions to the people you admire or read biographies as inspiration.

4. Remind yourself nobody is perfect.

There is important to remember that nobody is perfect, and nobody is living a painless life. Any triumph requires an obstacle to be overcome. And everybody is fighting on their own, whether you are close enough to know it or not.

5. Appreciate.

There may be times when competition is appropriate, but your job is not one of them. We have all been thrown together at this same moment on this exact planet. And the sooner we stop competing against others to "win," the faster we can start working together to realize it. Therefore, the first and most crucial step in overcoming the habit of competition is to routinely appreciate and compliment the contribution of others.

6. Practice gratitude.

Gratitude always focuses on recognizing the good things we already have in our world.

7. See your own successes.

Whether you are a doctor, writer, musician, landscaper, housewife, or student—you have a unique perspective backed by unique experiences and unique gifts. You can love, serve, and contribute. You have everything you need to accomplish good in our world. So, with that opportunity squarely in front of you, become intimately aware of your past successes. And find motivation in them to pursue more good changes.

8. Desire the greater qualities in your life.

Some of the greatest treasures in this world are hidden from sight: love, humility, empathy, generosity, and many others. Among these higher qualities, there is no measurement. So desire them above everything else and remove yourself from society's definition of success.

9. Compare with yourself.

We ought to strive to be the best possible versions of ourselves—not only for our own selves but for the benefit and contribution we can offer to the world. So work hard to take care of yourself physically, emotionally, and spiritually. Commit to growing a little bit each day of your life. And learn to celebrate the even minor advancements you are making without comparing them to others.

With so many harmful effects inherent in comparison, it is a shame we ever take part in it. But this struggling is real for most of us. Fortunately, it does not need to be, and now we know how to change our perspectives. As a result, the freedom found in comparing less is entirely worth the effort.

CHAPTER 35: WHY HELPING OTHERS SUCCEED CAN BE YOUR GREATEST SUCCESS

O ur greatest successes in life are often found in helping others succeed. And our most lasting and fulfilling achievements are often earned by helping others fulfill theirs.

> *"It is not true that nice guys finish last.*
> *Nice guys are winners before the game*
> *ever starts."* — *Addison Walker*

This is foreign thinking to a culture that often sees the world as one big competition. In people's minds, there is a set number of winners and losers. And if somebody else wins, that's one less opportunity for me to be successful.

I have come to realize the mindset of competition is based on a faulty premise. It assumes there is a finite-sized pie—that one more success in another's life equals one less success in mine. But quite frankly, this approach is incorrect.

There is a wonderful freedom in realizing the size of the pie is not finite—that in reality, the pie keeps growing. And another's success does not mean I have less opportunity. In fact, another's a success can actually be my success if I had an opportunity to enable, encourage, and promote them along the way.

Consider how helping another achieve success results in significant benefits in a number of directions:

* The receivers have reached a far greater potential than they could have on their own.

* The givers are remembered fondly and are often publicly (and privately) thanked for their contribution.

* Our world has been bettered and has been given a

life-giving model to emulate.

* And the cycle begins again.

Now, just to be clear, I am starting with an assumption that our greatest joys in life are rarely found in the relentless pursuit of selfish ambition. I mean that selfish desires always leave us searching for more.

Inherently, we all know we have been designed to live for something greater than ourselves. So our contribution to this world has to be measured by something more meaningful than the size of our house. And our lives are going to find lasting significance in how we choose to live and how we enable to live others.

CHAPTER 36: SOMETIMES IT IS IMPORTANT TO SAY "NO" AT WORK

Saying "no" could be one of the most important skills you need at work right now. The majority of people I've spoken to recently are at some extreme level of busyness. Maybe so busy that the word "busy" doesn't fit them anymore. "Super busy" has become the next stage of acceptance and possibly the newest trend.

What this busyness says to me is that a lot of us are finding it difficult to say "no" at work. We've got accustomed to playing catch up and wrestling with a thousand and one things to do. It's quickly becoming normal to be overwhelmed with stuff to do. But when you stop and think about it, that's not normal.

So why do we find using this tiny two-letter word such a difficult skill to perfect? Because saying "no" stirs up intensely negative emotions—embarrassment and guilt.

In a recent study, a group of people was each loaned a book from the library and then instructed to deface it. Half of the people were said that it felt wrong to do, but they did it anyway. It was later discovered that those people who chose to deface the book found it so difficult to reject the person who had asked.

Our history shows that humans found considerable benefits being in groups, notably hunting and staying alive. Being in a group increased our chances of survival with the ability to share resources. With time acceptance was seen as a survival mechanism, and therefore saying no makes us think we'll be perceived negatively, and as a result, excluded.

Something within us likes to create and sustain connections with others, and anything that threatens to break that bond will cause us to worry. Saying "no" to joining a meeting, not helping someone when they have asked for it, or turning down an invitation creates a sense of panic, so, in the end, we take the easy way out, the path of least resistance. And then, before we know it, we've become overwhelmed under a massive pile of "yes."

But there's another thing to consider here also— our own desire to be seen to always be doing stuff. Busyness is becoming an addictive culture, and there is still a large part of us that wants to be seen as in demand or needed (which raises our perceived level of importance).

But how do we get out of this vicious circle? Let's figure it out:

Ask Questions and re-prioritize

Some bosses don't really know the intricacies of the tasks that are going on within their teams. It's not their job to know all the ins and outs, but it is their job to move obstacles out of the way so you can be successful. You do, however, need to tell them when you've hit your limit.

So when you get another request from your boss to do something, and you are already at capacity, ask them what the priority is just now. If you take on this new task, maybe one of the older things you're working on is not as important anymore?

Empower others

Have colleagues become reliant on you without even knowing it? Are they calling you before even trying to figure things out for themselves? Are you rescuing them because you feel you need to?

Sometimes helping behaviors can trigger dopamine, serotonin, and oxycontin, a neurochemical cocktail that makes us feel good for a short time. Seeing people flourish and feeling satisfied that we have provided good advice—it's only momentarily gratifying. Moreover, giving advice and getting hooked on always being the one to rescue can be an occupational problem.

The effects of you always helping and say "yes" everywhere can cause severe long-term damage to others, and we may not even see it. But, conversely, one person's inability to say "no" can bring the whole team or organization crashing down.

Sometimes we just can't help but want to fix everything for people, and their tasks become a burden for us. As a result, you're overpromising but can't keep your word, and the relationships you worked so hard to build are becoming strained.

If the relationship is strong, the person receiving the "no" will understand, be empathetic to your mounting commitments and help you by giving you the space you need. But we believe others will judge us more harshly than they actually do. In reality, most people are so caught up in their own world, with their own mounting list of things, that they would have probably forgotten about your answer and moved on to something else.

Cultivate a Joy of Missing Out (JOMO)

The fear of missing out is such a pull that we can say "yes" to all sorts of things. There is a lot of social pressure connected with super busyness as well as the perceived sense of duty to do things like answer emails at any time. But our desire to get ahead mixed with social media addiction has ended up growing the emotionally intelligent antidote—The Joy Of Missing Out (JOMO). JOMO is a concept originally related to deterring the scrolling on our phones and the need to fit in. But this approach can also be used in work.

Being okay with not knowing everything, being everywhere, or seeing everyone grants you the ability to be more present and understand your own capacity. JOMO helps us to phase out the "should" and become more intentional with our time. It allows us to focus where we are needed on the most important things. As a bi-product, we can spend less time being anxious or competitive and receive back our energy.

So my advice for you now is to have courage, to be brave, and say "no" at least one thing this week. Getting better at saying "no" will not just be good for you—it will be good for your relationships, and it will be good for business.

CHAPTER 37:
10 SIMPLE WAYS TO HELP YOU SAY NO

Sometimes it's very hard to say no, especially at work. It can feel very uncomfortable. You might feel like you are letting colleagues down. Even so, it's one of the most important ways to create the space you want for what matters most. Not only do we need time to do the usual thousand things, but we deserve time to engage in the things that are on our heart lists, not just the things on our to-do lists. This is the things like:

* Disconnecting from the internet for one day

* Calling friend who makes you laugh

* Taking a long walk

* Doodling in a notebook

* Laying around with your feet up

* Relaxing

It takes time to take care of ourselves. And when we don't take that time, it's hard to take care of anyone else, at least not for very long. So continuing to serve everyone but ourselves will leave us completely depleted, and there will be consequences.

Saying no isn't easy, especially for kind, generous souls and for people who are used to saying "yes" to everything.

"Yes, I'll meet that deadline."

"Yes, I'll answer every email."

"Yes, I'll take that call."

"Yes, I'll meet you for lunch."

"Yes, I'll make a wonderful dinner."

"Yes, I'll drive you to the airport."

"Yes, I'll make that thing."

"Yes, I'll respond to everything that annoys me on social media."

The list goes on and on and on. But let me advise 10 simple ways to help you say "no" to people correctly:

1. Solve your issues first.

If the first thing you do in the office is solving other people's problems, you may never have a chance to solve your issues. So first sort out your issues, and then intervene in others.

2. Figure out what matters to you by asking questions.

It may sound ridiculous, but it helps to ask the questions out loud. So put your hands on your heart and ask:

"Does this really matter to me?"

"Am I holding on for the right reasons?"

"Is this good for me and to my health?"

"Is this contributing to the life I want or to the way I want to treat people?"

Ask it about your work, about how you feel, about your stuff, about invitations, requests, and everything. Just put your hands on your heart and ask. Your heart knows things, and it will help you make space for what matters most.

3. Don't say "yes" when your heart says "no."

We've all said "yes" when we wanted to say "no." Whether we say it out of guilt, for fear of missing out, or out of habit, it's important to note that saying "yes" when your heart says "no" is a disservice not only to you but to everyone you say "yes" to. If your gut says "no," it will fight the "yes" all the way through. You won't give your best, and you may end up resenting the person who asked you to commit. As a result, you won't be excited to contribute. So don't suppress yourself.

4. Trust your intuition.

When deciding whether to commit to something, if you feel anything less than, "It's a good idea!" then answer "no." When you say "no" to not-so-good ideas, you leave space in your life for perfect ideas.

5. Make a decision quickly.

If it's impossible for you to say "no" or know when to say "no" or how to say "no," make a decision very quickly. Make a commitment to say "no" without a doubt to every unimportant request for 21 days. Then, practice the loving "no" over and over again. Finally, share your challenge with others, not as a built-in excuse, but to inspire them to respect their own time and what matters to them too.

6. Be clear (with yourself and people).

Saying things like, "let me think about it," is often a delay tactic. When you know it's a no, say "no." If you want to say "yes," just say it. Be clear with yourself and the people around you.

7. Know you can be grateful while saying "no."

For a moment picturing yourself spending all the time, you've now freed up doing the thing that really matters to you before responding with your "no." Then ask yourself:

"How can I be kind and respectful yet also stand strong in what I need?"

"What would that sound like?"

Even by telling people "no," you can still be a good, well-mannered person. Just speak to people respectfully.

8. Keep it short.

"No" is a complete sentence. Expand when you need to, but still, keep it short. Then, in just a few sentences, you can say "no" with gratitude.

"No, thank you. I appreciate you thinking of me, but I have another commitment."

This is better than a long explanation about how busy and sorry you are.

9. Let go of the guilt.

Believe in yourself and what you know is best for your life, and say "no" to guilt. But, of course, you will help someone in their time of need, so dump the guilt around not attending every event or picking someone up from the airport at midnight.

10. Turn off FOMO (Fear of Missing out) mode.

Instead of feeling like you are missing out on something else, honor the opportunities you make to yourself. For example, when you decline an invitation, find joy in how you decide to spend your time instead of wondering what you missed out on. Feel the joy that you have a choice and joy because you are protecting what matters most.

When all of your free time and space is dedicated to keeping up, catching up, regrouping, and making ends meet—it's not free time. So if you really want free time or if you crave a full night of sleep, a proper lunch break, or at least 24 hours away from your email—you are going to have to say "no" a lot.

If we want better serve the world, we must have time to respond thoughtfully instead of reacting when we are tired and overwhelmed. When you sit quietly and put your hands on your heart, you'll know what matters for you and the people around you most.

CHAPTER 38: TRUTHS THAT WILL BRING PEACE WHEN YOU DEAL WITH DIFFICULT BOSS

S uppose you've been feeling drained by your regular encounters with a difficult boss. In that case, I urge you to gradually implement and practice the strategies I've outlined below (one at a time). Then, as you're doing this, remind yourself not to engage in this person's negative behavior. Don't get sucked in— keep your composure, and save your inner peace. And do so until these truths become deeply rooted in your consciousness.

12 Truths That Will Bring Peace When You Deal with Difficult Boss:

1. Be mindful. The greatest stress you go through when dealing with a difficult boss is not fueled by the words or actions of this person. It is fueled by your mind giving his words and actions importance.

2. Remember that what others say and do and the opinions they have are based almost entirely on their self-reflection. So don't take things personally. Instead of getting angry over the words of your boss, choose to grow stronger because of him.

3. Let the opinions of others inform you, but don't let them limit you. Don't let anyone's drama, ignorance, hate, or negativity stop you from being yourself. If you find yourself constantly trying to prove your worth to others, you've already forgotten your true value. So take a deep breath, and do what you know is right.

4. Gossip end at a wise person's ears. Be wise and seek to understand before you attempt to judge. Use your judgment not as a weapon for putting others down but as a tool for making positive choices that help you build your own character.

5. It's okay sometimes to be upset. But it's never okay to be cruel. Rage, hate, and resentment do not change the hearts of others—they only change yours.

6. Forgive others. Do it not because they deserve forgiveness, but because you deserve peace. So free yourself of the burden of being an eternal victim.

7. Stay positive even when negativity surrounds you. Smile when others suppress laughter. It's the easiest way to make a difference in the world around you.

8. Don't expect to see positive changes in your life if you constantly surround yourself with difficult colleagues and bosses. The great danger of being around a difficult community too often is that you start to become like it without even knowing it. On the other hand, just because you are kind and respectful to someone does not mean you have to spend extra time with them. So be mindful of the daily community you keep.

9. Always set a good example. Treat everyone with kindness and respect, even those who are rude to you. Do it not because they are nice, but because you are. And do your best to be thankful for a rude and difficult boss, too, because he serves as a great reminder of how not to be.

10. The way we treat people we strongly disagree with is a test of what we've learned about love, compassion, and kindness. Life is too beautiful to argue and fight. So value the people who matter and move on from the drama with your head held high.

11. If you really want to be peaceful, then stop being afraid of being yourself, and stop thinking every second about what others think of you. We can't give what we don't have. So instead, experience life on your terms, and you'll be life-giving to others.

12. Make it a daily ritual to work hard in silence, do what you have to do, and ignore the drama, discouragement, and negativity surrounding you. Let your consciousness be your compass.

Sometimes we need to be reminded to actually practice the little habits that allow us to better understand and nurture the right bonds or let go of the wrong ones. We need to be reminded to be selective in our community, too. And then, step by step, everything will fall into place.

CHAPTER 39:
COMMON LIES
THAT KEEP OUR
SCHEDULES
OVERWHELMED

The speed of our world is constantly increasing. Technology and communication continue to improve and change our lives. Information moves faster and faster. Social media rewards those who never turn it off.

Demands, expectations, and accessibility continue to expand, but the number of hours in a week does not. As a result, our overwhelmed lives get busier and busier. Even worse, we are unable to identify the hidden mistruths in our hearts that are contributing to the problem.

This approach to life rarely benefits us in the long run because a busy life is an unreflective life. In fact, very often, we are so busy scurrying from one thing to another we don't even have the space to realize our schedules have become overwhelmed. As a result, we don't recognize how our overcommitted lives are harming the people around us and, of course, us.

I suggest you consider 10 hidden lies that keep our schedules overwhelmed:

1. Everything is important.

Our world has a tendency to make everything appear urgent, meaningful, and beneficial to our lives. As the speed of information increases, our minds are seemingly less equipped to filter all the opportunities. But the most productive among us realize that nobody can accomplish everything. They are relentless in their understanding of mission and the reality that only a few things are truly important. So they never sacrifice the important for the trivial.

2. I'm more productive if I'm busy.

Maybe you can be more productive for a short while, but human beings are not designed to work relentlessly without periods of good rest. Countless studies confirm the importance of rest for focus and productivity. Eventually, a lifestyle of busyness will detract from our goals (and, more importantly, from our well-being).

3. Money will bring fulfillment.

We often get caught up in needless busyness because of our desire to earn more money. Ever notice how often we are offered money for our time? While it is important to work hard and provide for your family's needs, it isn't very smart to think money is the quickest shortcut to a better living.

4. Accolades always bring fulfillment.

The thinking goes like this: The busier we are, the more we can accomplish, and the more respect we can earn. And the more respect and accolades we receive, the more we can surely prove our worth to others. Unfortunately, if you are trying to find fulfillment in someone else's opinion of you, you will never find it. You will always be left searching and working for more.

5. I am needed.

Pride is defined as holding an excessively high opinion of oneself and one's importance. And it leads to overwhelmed schedules because of the wrong thinking that follows it: "Nobody else can do what I do." This pride affects the way we view our business, our work, our family, and our relationships. Left unchecked, it leads to a busy life and, in the end, a fall.

6. Busy makes me look more important.

Busy is not a badge of honor. On the contrary, being busy doing the wrong things is actually quite unattractive. Just remember, in a society rushing to keep up with everyone else, those who find peace, contentment, and rest are the ones admired.

7. I need to be busy to keep up with everyone else.

Modern people are frantically trying to earn enough to buy things they are too busy to enjoy. So it may seem that the only way to get ahead in life is to outwork everyone else. But just because everyone else appears busy does not mean they are busy with the right things. Nor does it mean they are finding happiness in their pursuits.

8. I don't have a choice.

Many of us live over-busy lives because of the expectations and demands of other people. In these cases, it is very important to remember you always have a choice. Sure, there are seasons of life that require more of your energy and time than others —but seasons always change. If your seasons of life haven't changed recently, you may need to revisit who is making the decisions in your life and where you can regain some of your control.

9. Quietness is laziness.

Very often, people avoid dealing with life's deeper issues by packing their schedules tight. Someone who is discontent with their life's choices can escape the difficult thoughts by masking them with busyness. In such cases, quietness is very important. Sometimes quietness is hard but always worth the effort. And quietness is not laziness.

10. Being busy is a good example for children.

We often think that being constantly busy means setting a good example for children. We believe that in this way we will teach children to be hardworking. But in reality, everything is not so simple. For example, if parents are too busy to spend time with their children, then their children begin to seek the attention of others. And what they find isn't always a good example to follow.

Many of the lies we have been told since childhood crowd out the things in life that matter most. As a result, instead of enjoying the benefit of peaceful, intentional living, we hurry from one needless triviality to another. From today, don't ever get so busy chasing the wrong things that you miss enjoying the right things. Live in balance.

THE 5TH SIMPLE STEP TO YOUR PERFECT HOM...

CHAPTER 40: A HELPFUL GUIDE TO BECOMING UNBUSY

B usy has become the new fine. As in, when you ask somebody how they were doing, they used to answer, "Thank you, I am fine." But nowadays, everybody just answers, "Busy."

Seemingly, busy has become the default state for too many of our lives. But is the state of being busy really improving our lives? Certainly not.

Statistics indicate 33% of Americans are living with extreme stress daily.

75% of parents are too busy even to read to their children at night.

Nearly 50% of Americans say they regularly lie

awake at night because of stress.

This is a problem—we have become too busy. But in reality, it doesn't have to be this way.

> *"Those who are wise won't be busy, and those who are too busy can't be wise."* — *Lin Yutang*

Each of us can take intentional steps to unbusy our schedules and lives. So consider this helpful guide to becoming unbusy:

1. Realize that being busy is a choice.

It is a decision we all make. We are rarely forced into a lifestyle of busyness. So the first and most crucial step to becoming less busy is to simply realize that only we determine our schedules. And we do have a choice in the matter.

2. Revisit your priorities and responsibilities.

Become more intentional with your priorities and responsibilities in life. Determine the most significant contributions you can offer this world and schedule your time around those first. Busyness is, at its core, about misplaced priorities.

3. Appreciate and schedule rest.

One of the reasons many of us keep busy schedules is we fail to recognize the value of good rest. But good rest is beneficial to our bodies, our minds, and our souls. So set aside one day per week for rest. Intentionally schedule it on your calendar and then guard it at all costs.

4. Own fewer possessions.

The things we own take up far more space, time, and mental energy than we realize. They need to be cleaned, organized and maintained. As a result, the more we own, the more time is required. Own less stuff and find more time because of it.

5. Stop the glorification of busyness.

Busy, in and of itself, is not a badge of true honor. In fact, directed at the wrong pursuits, it is actually limiting to our full potential. Therefore, it is okay not to be busy.

6. Cultivate space in your working routine.

Find time in your morning to sit quietly before starting your day. Take enough time for lunch. Invest your time and energy in reading or sport. Find opportunities for breaks at work in between projects. Begin right away to cultivate a few moments of freedom in your busy working day.

7. Find power in the word "no."

Everybody agrees that no one pursuit can be successfully followed by a man who is preoccupied with many things. Recognize the inherent power in the word "no." Learning to say "no" to less important events opens your life to pursue the most important.

Busy does not need to define us. Unbusy is possible for everyone. It's okay to be happy with a calm, steady life. So what are you going to do after reading this chapter?

CHAPTER 41: COMPELLING REASONS TO SCHEDULE MORE NOTHING

I t seems as if there is always more to do. So doing nothing can feel like a luxury we can't afford. Even with schedule changes, we still manage to fill our days with more to-dos. Unfortunately, when we refuse to do nothing, we compromise everything.

People can do so much doing before their bodies say "enough" and "break down." And this break down might not be obvious or dramatic, but people lose focus, feel exhausted and struggle to be inspired and motivated. And then they think that they are supposed to feel like this because there is so much to do, and the cycle repeats. But slowing down and doing nothing is a chance to find rest, renewal, and delight.

Now, consider 3 compelling reasons to schedule more nothing:

1. Free time makes room to handle emergencies better.

People plan their days, hour by hour. They don't leave any room in between tasks, appointments, or commitments. As a result, emergencies and sur-prises consider this an invitation to show up and blow up the notion that you think you run the world. So create margin and leave a little room for nothing in your schedule. Nothing may turn into something, and you'll have time for it. If nothing is nothing, consider it bonus time for a nap, a walk, or just sitting quietly with your thoughts.

2. Time for nothing invites you to remember yourself.

Doing nothing allows you to listen to your heart and process ideas and emotions. After a day of non-stop input, you have to recover. So, schedule noth-ing if only to give yourself a few moments to re-member who you are, what you want, and how you want to live.

3. Less rushing around makes you a kinder person.

Compare how you feel coming home after a day of back-to-back meetings with how you feel after coming home after the normal working day. Consider how you treat people after constantly reacting to email, social media, and people you work with versus how you treat people after you've unplugged for a while and given yourself time to be alone, away from people and digital devices. You are likely more present, focus, softer, and kinder.

If doing nothing is hard for you, consider the benefits above. Pause is restorative for your mind, body, and heart. It's a gift to you and affects everyone around you.

BONUS CHAPTER: REMAIN CALM EVEN WHEN OTHERS ARE OUT OF CONTROL

As human beings, we all have an idea in our heads about how things are supposed to be. As a result, we all get frustrated when things don't play out the way we expect them to, and people don't behave like they're "supposed" to. For example, we expect our spouses and children to act a certain way, our friends to be kind and agreeable, strangers to be less difficult, and so on and so forth. Sadly, this is what often messes our relationships up the most.

When reality hits us, and everyone seems to be

doing the opposite of what we want them to do, we overreact—anger, frustration, arguments, tears, and stress. But what can we do about this? Deep breath and let go.

You can't control how other people behave and think. You even can't control everything that happens to you. What you really can control is how you respond to it all. In your response is your true power.

So when you feel like your nerves are about to blow —take a long, deep breath. Deep breathing calms down our fight-or-flight reactions, releases tension, and allows us to quiet our anxious nerves. As a result, we can choose more considerate and constructive responses, no matter the situation. Just try.

There's no doubt that it can drive us crazy when we don't get what we expect from people (especially when they are rude and difficult). But trying to change the unchangeable, wanting other people to be exactly the way we want them to be, just doesn't work.

The alternative, though, is unthinkable to most of us: To breathe and let go. This is how we can lead by example and accept people even when they irritate us.

Here are some ways of being calm during the working day:

* At least one time during your day, take one deep breath, inhaling through the nose and exhaling through the mouth.

* Let go of the ideals and expectations you have about others that cause unnecessary frustration, arguments, and bouts of anger.

* Remind yourself that you can't control other people.

* Give people empathy and space.

* Remind yourself that other people can handle their lives however they choose.

* See the good in them.

* Remember that when others are being difficult, they are often going through a difficult time you know nothing about.

* Don't take their behavior personally.

Being this way takes practice—but it's worth it. It helps us be more mindful, makes us less frustrated, lowers our stress, improves our relationships, and allows us to make the world a slightly more peaceful place to be.

If you're ready to feel more peace and less inner angst, I share with you some principles I've learned to remain calm and centered, even when those around me can't seem to contain themselves. These principles reinforce the bullet points above, and when you consistently practice them, the world within you and around you becomes a lot easier to cope with.

So, let's practice together:

1. Create a morning ritual that starts your day right.

Don't rush into your day by checking your phone and email. Don't put yourself in a stressful state of mind from the very beginning of the day. Instead, create time and space for a morning ritual that's focused and peaceful.

Here's an example: As soon as you get out of bed, take five deep breaths inhaling through the nose and exhaling through the mouth (you can also do this while lying or sitting). As a result, when you begin your day mindfully, you lay the foundation for the whole day to be calm and centered, regardless of what's going on around you.

I challenge you to try this—start small, with just five deep breaths a day. Do this for twenty-one days. After twenty-one days, if this daily ritual becomes easy, add another five breaths in the evening.

2. Get comfortable with pausing.

Don't imagine the worst when you just encounter a little drama. So when someone is acting irrationally, don't join them by rushing to make a negative judgment call. Instead, pause. Instead, take a deep breath.

Sometimes even good people behave poorly under stress. Don't you? But when you pause, it gives you space to realize your thoughts. And it also allows the other person the space to take a deep breath with you. In most cases, that extra time and space are all we need.

3. Talk less and learn to appreciate silence.

Don't fall into unnecessary arguments just because you feel uncomfortable in silence. Don't say things you'll regret a few minutes later just to fill your eardrums with noise. You can choose your response to momentary discomfort with silence. Just inhale. Then exhale. A moment of silence in a moment of uncomfortable can save you from a hundred moments of regret.

4. Respect people's differences.

Learn to respect the opinions of other people. Just because someone does it differently doesn't make it wrong! There are many roads to what's right in our world. Everyone is entitled to their own opinion and path. So choose your actions wisely.

It is absolutely possible to appreciate the company of someone you don't completely agree with. However, when you make a commitment to remain neutral on topics that don't matter that much or speak respectfully about your disagreements, both parties can remain calm and move forward pleasantly.

5. Don't take people's behavior personally.

If you take everything personally, you will be offended every day. But there's no reason for it. You may not be able to control all the things people say and do to you. But you can decide not to be worried about their behavior. So make that decision for yourself today.

There is a huge amount of freedom that comes when you detach from other people's beliefs and behaviors. The way people treat you is their problem. But how you react is yours.

Do you know that everyone behaves the way they behave based on how they feel inside? Unfortunately, some people never learn how to cope with their stressful emotions effectively. When someone is acting obnoxious, it's vital that you remain calm inside you, no matter what. Don't allow others to knock you off your center. That's where your most incredible power lies.

6. Be compassionate.

In the busyness of today's world, people tend to be fearful, worried, hurting, and distracted about everything (even about the smallest things). But when you can put yourself in the other person's shoes, you give them the space to regroup without putting any extra pressure on them.

Remember, we never know what's really going on in someone's private life. So when you interact with others in stressful environments, set an intention to be supportive by leaving the expectations, demands, and judgments at the door.

7. Extend generosity.

Everyone can be upset and lose their temper sometimes. Remind yourself: We are all more alike than we are different.

When you catch yourself passing expectations, add "just like me sometimes" to the end of a sentence. For example:

* He is rude, just like me sometimes.

* She is so impatient, just like me sometimes.

* That person is grouchy, just like me sometimes.

Then choose to let things go.

8. Use healthy choices and alternatives.

When we face stressful situations, we often soothe ourselves with unhealthy choices—eating sugary snacks, drinking alcohol, smoking, etc. Sometimes it's easy to respond to anger with unhealthy distractions.

From today, notice how you cope with stress. Then replace bad habits with healthy habits. For example, take a walk in the park. Write something in your journal. Make a cup of tea and sit quietly. Listen to pleasant music. Talk with a close friend. Remember: healthy habits make happy people.

9. Remind yourself of what's good.

At the end of the day, reflect on your small daily wins and all the little things that are going well. Count even small events on your fingers that happened during the day that you're undoubtedly grateful for. And promise yourself to do more of these things.

Keeping positive in mind helps you move beyond the negativity around you. So let your positivity empower you to think kindly of others, speak kindly to others, and do kind things for others. Kindness always makes things better.

10. Create more good it in the world.

Create the outcomes that others might be grateful for at the end of their day. Be a part of what's good in this world. And keep doing your job well.

The most fundamental aggression to ourselves and others—the most fundamental harm we can do to human nature as a whole—is to remain ignorant by not having the awareness to look at ourselves and others honestly and gently. So take a deep breath. And the next. And another one.

Although this is the last chapter of this book—
a new chapter of your life is just beginning!

If you want more, I recommend other
books in the *5 Steps* series.

I will see you there.

YOUR OPINION MATTERS

"The 5th Simple Step to Your Perfect Home, Job, and Life" book took me hundreds of inspiring hours to write it. And I sincerely hope this book helps you to achieve your goals.

Now, let me ask you for help. Please take a minute to review this book on *Amazon*. It will significantly help me on my writing journey:

https://www.amazon.com/dp/B08XXNQ5LC

Regards,

Ivan

ALSO BY IVAN KUZNIETSOV

Here is a list of countries where you can buy eBooks by Ivan Kuznetsov:

United States

United Kingdom

Canada

Australia

Germany

France

Spain

Italy

Netherlands

Brazil

Mexico

India

Japan

**<u>All eBooks are *Amazon* exclusives and
are available for free with a Kindle
Unlimited membership!</u>**

Non-fiction:

5 STEPS

The 1st Simple Step to Your Perfect Home: How
to Methodologically Sort Through All Items,
Keep Important, and Get Rid of Unnecessary

The 2nd Simple Step to Your Perfect Home: How
to Methodically Put All Necessary Items in the
Optimal Places and Organize Everyday Life

The 3rd Simple Step to Your Perfect Home: How to
Mindfully Clean Your House, Digital, Mind, and Life

The 4th Simple Step to Your Perfect Home:
How to Turn Your House Cleaning Routine
into a Joyful Family Tradition

The 5th Simple Step to Your Perfect Home, Job,
and Life: How Less Becomes More at Work

MINDFUL MOMENTS COLLECTION

The Mindful Thrift: How to Appreciate What
We Have and Save What We Do Not Notice

The Mindful Nutrition: How to Enjoy the True
Taste of Food, Have a Slim Body and 33 (+3) Home
Cooking Recipes for a Delicious Degustation

The Mindful Eating for Beginners: Step-by-Step Guide for Lifelong Health and Collection of Quick & Easy Recipes for Every Day

Fiction:

BIG LITTLE STORIES

Escape to Myself

Sea Soul

The Mountain of Desires

An Epidemic 1,000 Years Before Us

The information above is current as of August 2021. For more information about the latest books, visit the Ivan Kuznietsov author page:

www.amazon.com/author/kuznietsov_ivan

ABOUT THE AUTHOR

Ivan Kuznietsov is a certified World Class Manufacturing (WCM/Lean) Instructor. He studied extensively at various universities and now coaches how to consistently and methodically integrate the best Lean practices to both business processes and everyday life. Together with the team, Ivan reached the Silver Award for World Class Manufacturing system implementation in 2017.

In addition to coaching, Ivan is an author of the "5 Steps" book series. In each book, he explains in simple words how to mindfully use helpful Lean tools (such as the Root Cause Analysis, Standardized Work, 5S System, etc.) to improve the quality of work and daily life. Ivan writes books with one simple aim in mind: To show people that Lean thinking is not just a methodology but a modern lifestyle.

As a hobby, Ivan is an author of two other book

series: "Big Little Stories" and "Mindful Moments Collection." He writes those book series to provide the readers with the inspiration to change.

Amazon Author Page — www.amazon.com/author/kuznietsov_ivan

Goodreads — www.goodreads.com/kuznietsov_ivan

Facebook — www.facebook.com/kuznietsov.ivan

Instagram — www.instagram.com/kuznietsov_ivan/

Twitter — twitter.com/kuznietsov_ivan

LinkedIn — www.linkedin.com/in/kuznietsov-ivan

Email — kuznietsov.ivan.post@gmail.com

ACKNOWLEDG-
MENTS

I want to thank all the people who contributed to this book and supported me on this writing journey. Although I do not mention the names of each of you, you can feel my gratitude. And I also want to thank you, dear reader, for choosing this book from among the millions in existence. Thank you for your trust!

NOTES

1. Mintzberg, H. (1973). The Nature of Managerial Work. New York: Harper and Row.

2. Stewart, R. (1967). Managers and Their Jobs. London: Macmillan.

3. Karr-Wisniewski, P., & Lu, Y. (2010). When more is too much: Operationalizing technology overload and exploring its impact on knowledge worker productivity. Computers in Human Behavior 26, 1061–72.

4. Stephens, J. P., Heaphy, E., & Dutton, J. E. (2011). High-quality connections. In The Oxford Handbook of Positive Organizational Scholarship (385–99); Dutton, J. E. (2006). Energize Your Workplace: How to Create and Sustain High-Quality Connections at Work. John Wiley & Sons.

5. O'Brien, Katharine Ridgway. "Just Saying 'No': An Examination of Gender Differences in the Ability to Decline Requests in the Workplace." PhD diss., Rice University, 2014. https://hdl.handle.net/1911/77421 (accessed 12/11/19).

Printed in Great Britain
by Amazon